INANNA
Lady of Largest Heart

Poems of the
Sumerian High Priestess

ENHEDUANNA

Foreword by Judy Grahn

by Betty De Shong Meador

University of Texas Press, Austin

INANNA

Lady of Largest Heart

Poems of the
Sumerian High Priestess
ENHEDUANNA

Copyright © 2000 by Betty De Shong Meador
Foreword copyright © 2000 by the University of Texas Press
All rights reserved
Printed in the United States of America
First edition, 2000
Requests for permission to reproduce material from this work should be
sent to Permissions, University of Texas Press, P.O. Box 7819, Austin, TX
78713-7819.
♾ The paper used in this book meets the minimum requirements of
ANSI/NISO Z39.48-1992 (R1997) (Permanence of Paper).
Library of Congress Cataloging-in-Publication Data
Enheduanna.
Inanna, Lady of Largest Heart : poems of the high priestess Enheduanna /
[edited] by Betty De Shong Meador.— 1st ed.
p.   cm.
ISBN 0-292-75241-5 (cloth : alk. paper) —
ISBN 0-292-75242-3 (pbk. : alk. paper)
1. Sumerian poetry—Translations into English.   2. Sumerian poetry—
History and criticism.   3. Inanna (Sumerian deity)—Poetry.   I. Meador,
Betty De Shong, 1931–   II. Title.
PJ4083 .E54   2000   899'.951—dc21   00-036407

To Mel

Table of Contents

⌄⌄

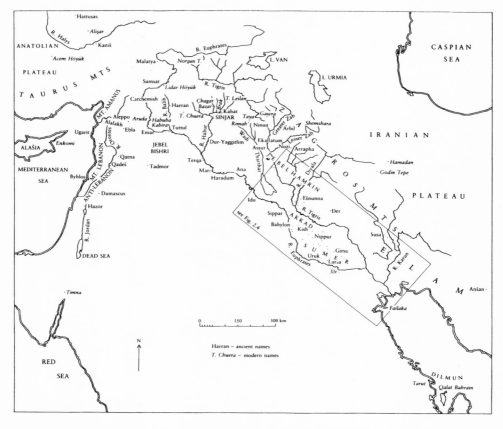

1. Map of the Near East 3200–1600 B.C.E. *Courtesy of International Thomson Publishing Services.*

Foreword

Enheduanna's
Forty-Fourth Century

Judy Grahn

In the mid 1980s I taught writing classes for women. Betty De Shong Meador entered my life in 1984. She had requested a teacher who could work with "elements of the dark"—meaning destructive as well as constructive forces. Meador had already crafted a vigorous, poetically emphatic version of "The Descent Myth of the Goddess Inanna," and now wanted to take on the daunting task of translating Enheduanna, "the earliest known poet." At first she brought in tender lines and images, of Inanna as the bud of a flower. "Enheduanna was clearly in love with the goddess Inanna," she explained.

Week after week for several years, Meador arrived with her fresh translations, sparkling gifts that both inspired and riveted. Some parts were strange and at first utterly mysterious—the phrases of a poet whose name seemed unpronounceable . . . whose official position during her lifetime, "High Priestess of the Moon God of the city of Ur," seemed as exotic and far-removed as science-fiction fantasy. Some of the emerging phrases of this poet were provocative, baffling, and discomforting. The translator wondered, were they obsessional rants? Emotional fits? Were these only private emotings of a diary-keeper with an unknowable sensibility? But persistence is the mother of art, and finally the sinuous, breathtaking, full body of the howling, spitting, untamed goddess writhed completely into view.

Meador's initial witnesses sat shocked at the awesome raw power of the imagery—never in our experience associated with the feminine. At last, here it is—a philosophical story, told by a woman, and centering on the sacred, creative powers of the feminine. And it is a "dark" story indeed, quixotic in the many elements of life and death, sacred and profane—even qualities of gender itself are challenged and redefined in the hands of the High Priestess poet of Ur. In Meador's hands, Enheduanna's poetry is sure-voiced and inspired: clear, poignant, full of tensile strength, paying full tribute to the passion, power, and wisdom of the poet.

To place the Sumerian poet Enheduanna in a timeline, she lived seventeen hundred years before Sappho, eleven hundred before Homer, and just about five hundred before Abraham, if we place his birth at 1700 B.C.E. Enheduanna wrote her poetry very early in the evolution of writing, perhaps three hundred years after cuneiform vocabulary developed sufficiently to handle linguistic concepts. To have forty-five hundred lines from such an early writer—the mother of written poetry—is the pouring of fresh deep water into the well from which all writers drink.

Poet/priestess Enheduanna's geographical location—the city-states of the Tigris-Euphrates Valley—was known as "The Cradle of Civilization" in my grade school textbooks. Because of archaeological advances, we can say now that "civilization" is a moveable and constructed concept, that Africa is the likeliest "cradle" of culture, and that the material culture of skilled craftspeople can be dated at 40,000 B.P. or earlier. Nevertheless, the lavish crediting of origins to Mesopotamia was in recognition of mathematical, architectural, agricultural, and sociopolitical contributions that remain awe-inspiring. Ancient Sumer produced the earliest known writing, and with publication of *Inanna, Lady of Largest Heart,* we are privileged to meet the earliest known writer.

Great voices of the past have often emerged to lead literature forward in a procession that moves, paradoxically, century after century, backward in time. The relation between archaeology and literature has been reciprocal. Written accounts of Troy and Ur, for example, spurred archaeological digs at sites in Greece and Mesopotamia that confirmed the myths. In turn, archaeology deserves a Nobel Prize for its contribution to contemporary thought, pushing consciousness forward with each increasingly older discovery.

Poets especially have drawn from the emerging body of classical texts, which under the impetus of archaeological and folkloric discoveries, gradually spilled out from the earlier nexus of Roman and Greek to north and east with myths that were Norse, Persian, and Assyrian. Roman playwright Plautus, the publication of whose play *Menaechmi*, translated by one William Warner in 1594, just preceded the publication of *A Comedy of Errors*, supplied Shakespeare with the source material for his play. Generations of poets have drawn deeply from the well of ancient voices—Milton, Longfellow, Byron, Shelley, Poe, and dozens more relied on the legends of Ovid and Virgil, the plays and sagas of Euripides and Homer. By the 1898 edition of Thomas Bullfinch's *Age of Fable or Beauties of Mythology*, school children could also learn some rudiments from Egyptian, Mesopotamian, and Indian texts. These featured primarily masculine stories of the sun god Mithras and Hindu gods Brahman, Shiva, and Vishnu. But not only male writers benefited from emerging mythology; women writers, heartened by characters more vivid and far less guilty than Eve, freely incorporated ancient stories into their own emergent work.

With the recovery of Sappho, the classics from Greece produced a new wonder: a woman writer from antiquity. Her subjects were the gods, correct ritual, women, and love; her style was lyric. The primary goddess of Sappho's attention was the star goddess, Venus in Latin, Aphrodite in her native Greek tongue. Sappho was a teacher at a school for young women and a priestess, making her part of the female lineage of Enheduanna, priestess and devotee of the goddess identified with the planet Venus in her time: Astarte in Syrian, Ishtar in Akkadian, and Inanna in Sumerian.

In late nineteenth-century America, Emily Dickinson read from translations of the lyric fragments left to us by Sappho. Tragically, only one complete poem has been recovered since Sappho's work was burned early in the Christian era. The fragments that remain are quotes from later classical writers, or papyrus manuscripts excavated in Egypt. Yet even these fragments have had enormous impact.

Then, early in the twentieth century, the voice of the star goddess began to be heard with her own stories. At first this was only a murmur in Bulfinch's collection—under the heading "Phoenician Deities," goddess Astarte received a three-sentence mention as daughter of the moon. In 1913 Stephen Langdon published fragments of a lamentation from Mesopotamia; then translations of a goddess named Ishtar began to appear, about a descent she had made, a journey to the "netherworld." In 1930 translators startled the scholarly world with a Mesopotamian myth of a king, Gilgamesh, a historical figure, whose series of poems revealed themselves as a single epic. The fact that a flood myth was included in the episodes of the king's life created a stir of excitement—biblical texts had sources! The story told of the search by Gilgamesh to find new terms of immortality, and a rejection of the older philosophy of the goddess, Ishtar. But wait a minute—a goddess with a philosophy? This was news. What *was* her philosophy, and how did it differ from that embraced by Gilgamesh? Do these struggles have relevance to our own times?

Meantime, the Greek and Roman mythology so inspiring to pre-twentieth-century poets was colder on the tongues of twentieth-century women, who found Pandora's box of evils as blameful as Eve's apple. One small example suffices to show that the feminine has had little or no active principle in these myths. Samuel Coleridge's characterization of the sexes is typical: " 'Tis Jupiter who brings what e'er is great/and Venus who brings everything that's fair" (quoted in Bulfinch).

The psychological archetypes proved inadequate for women, who could not fit themselves into the small part played by Electra or the re-active vengeance of Clytemnestra or Medusa. Much richer and deeper archetypes were needed. Revisioning misogynist Greek mythology so her daughter could have positive empowering mythology, Charlene Spretnak (1975) drew from folklore, ritual, and her own imagination in recovering "lost" goddesses of pre-Hellenic Greece, searching for the undercurrent of the sacred feminine that Jane Ellen Harrison, Robert Graves, and others had insisted was real. Women craved points of view from that stream.

A multitude of twentieth-century writers have revised male-authored versions of women's myths, even though there simply was no original poetry from which to draw inspiration. Ignoring both myth and its ab-sence, Gertrude Stein reconstructed language to contain her own phi-losophy, while poet HD made intense collages of imagery of the sacred feminine to reconstruct Helen as a modern heroine, in *Helen in Egypt* (1961), a theme I took up in *The Queen of Wands* (1982). Native Ameri-can women such as Leslie Marmon Silko, Paula Gunn Allen, and Linda Hogan poured traditional stories into contemporary literary form, as did African Americans such as Luisah Teish and Audre Lorde. Diane DiPrima investigated Italian folklore to write her long chronicle of *Loba*.

Then in 1983, Inanna—the star goddess with her own voice and stories —burst full grown on the scene with a breathtaking complexity with the publication of *Inanna: Queen of Heaven and Earth,* the collaboration of a Sumerian scholar, Samuel Noah Kramer, and a popular dramatist, Diane Wolkstein. While Kramer had written on her earlier, the mix of scholastic translation and Wolkstein's poetic drama mirrored for modern women, who had been pouring into the workplace, a range of strengths, including sexual expression and autonomy, as they entered into science, spirits, artistic expression, political and economic power. Inanna celebrated her vulva, founded horticulture, and collected all the principles of her culture into her "boat of heaven." Her descent myth, assembled painstakingly from many fragments by Kramer, leaped into focus as a life journey with profound guidance for the choices women make and the circumstances of women's lives that demand surrender to a greater principle. In the Descent myth, that greater principle is also female. Suddenly the male-female schism of Greek myth is replaced by a "new" story; in this one, the feminine is not fractured, not dragged about in wars, not waiting, not "all that is fair," not killed by its own children, not cursed or reviled.

The reappearance of this germinative work at the turn of the millennium is particularly striking. Enheduanna's timing is impeccable. Here we are at the end of the twentieth century re-defining gender, deity, sexualities, theology, and the parameters of human hegemony. We struggle with the power of emotion to destroy our relationships, and the power of nature to destroy us, despite our fantasies of security. We struggle with inner and outer violence, how to survive loss with integrity, and how to have faith in something beyond humanity at a time when human capacity is expanding exponentially. These were some of Enheduanna's issues as well.

If the expansive progression "back to the future" continues, the next century will be storied in large measure by the literature of Mesopotamia, especially the myths of Inanna. With *Inanna, Lady of Largest Heart* we are given new philosophical depth that connects intricately with the lineage already in place. Biblical scholars will notice that Enheduanna's cry, "I am yours, why do you slay me?" precedes the similar cry of Job by nearly two thousand years, among other affinities with biblical texts. Scholars familiar with the oral literature of India's earth goddesses and of Kali will notice the overlap of characteristics, further affirming influence between India's Harappan and other Indus Valley cultures and the peoples of ancient Mesopotamia. Poets and other students of contemporary mythology may be astonished by a goddess whose powers

include smashing a mountain or changing someone's gender. Students of
the transgendering currently happening both socially and theologically
will find much to work with in Enheduanna's poetry.

When we consider the probable contribution of Enheduanna to bibli-
cal literature, we are confronted with a writer who may have influenced
an inestimable number of people over the centuries since her life. She
may well have "been with us since the beginning." When we further
consider Enheduanna's contributions to theology—that Meador demon-
strates so well—and that Enheduanna's descriptions of Inanna are the
oldest written litany of the characteristics of the active feminine principle
in nature—known as "Shakti" in India—the importance of the High
Priestess of Ur assumes far greater prominence than we ever could have
imagined for any individual writer.

We can now understand women's contribution to literature as both
germinal and having greatest-known longevity. Meador patiently takes
us through the strangeness of this territory, shows us how to slow down
to absorb the poetry, feel its greatness in ourselves, ponder the profun-
dity of the philosophy. Meador's interpretation is itself an injunction for
our age to reconnect fully with the mind of nature, that intelligent force
the Mayan people of Columbia call 'alana'—the mind inside nature—
and that the Sumerians called Inanna—Lady of Largest Heart.

Acknowledgments

∧ ⁄

The long period of germination that accompanies most books began with my search for Inanna before I knew of Enheduanna. My dear friends Gaye Williams and the late Maria Bowen, along with Carol Davis and others, created a performance of several of the Sumerian sacred marriage hymns, whose translation I had begun with Jerome Rothenberg. I remember our work with genuine gratitude. During this time I was fortunate to study with Diane di Prima in her "Hidden Religions" classes which gave dimension to the underground strand of a female-oriented spirituality. I thank her for her continued support. In the mid-1980s I began a women's writing group led by Judy Grahn. I am grateful to all the women who passed through these groups, for their considered critiques and encouragement. My collaboration with Judy Grahn is the solid alignment that keeps me on course. She is an indispensable mentor and sister-wayfarer.

My connection to Anne D. Kilmer, Assyriologist at the University of California, Berkeley, has been invaluable. She led me to Daniel A. Foxvog, generous and capable Sumerologist, with whom I studied a number of Sumerian texts, including the Enheduanna poems in this book. Professor Kilmer read more than one version of the manuscript, invited me into her classes, and freely answered my many questions. I am grateful to her graduate students John Carnahan and Mary Frances Wogec for their patient help and support.

I appreciate the numerous opportunities to present the work in progress, particularly at the C. G. Jung Institute of San Francisco and to audiences connected to Jung Societies throughout the country. I am especially grateful to Murray Stein and Chiron Publications for first publishing excerpts from Enheduanna's poetry. My colleagues Linda Leonard, Virginia Beane Rutter, Jean Kirsch, among others, have been consistently supportive. At the California Institute for Integral Studies (CIIS) and New College (San Francisco) and Pacifica Graduate Institute (Santa Barbara) I was given numerous opportunities to introduce to their challenging students the ideas in this book. My special thanks go to Elinor Gadon and the Women's Spirituality Program at CIIS.

The gracious acceptance of the manuscript by Jim Burr, my editor at University of Texas Press, created a welcome home for the book and for me a serendipitous homecoming to my alma mater. Marie Cantlon patiently edited the manuscript, and Sheryl Fullerton guided the process more than once.

Finally, with his cogent wisdom my husband and true companion, Mel Kettner, understood the meaning of the work from the beginning. My deepest gratitude to him who without flinching, endured the impact Enheduanna's ideas have had on our lives together.

INANNA

Lady of Largest Heart

Poems of the
Sumerian High Priestess

ENHEDUANNA

PART

I

The Cultural and Historical Context

Introduction
"Through the
Gate of Wonder" [1]

There are times when a person is seized by an idea or an event that grows into a living presence that makes demands on her or his life. Such was my experience when Inanna first appeared to me in a dream. Before the dream, I had never heard of this Sumerian goddess.

In the dream I am with a group of women who are preparing two graves. One is complete. Two tall sticks that curve into circles at the top are thrust into the soft dirt. Beside the stick figures is a bundle of palm fronds. The other grave is freshly dug. After the second body has been received and covered, we are to push similar stick figures into the soil and place a palm frond bundle beside them.

Two Jungian analysts, both alive at the time, are being buried. In my dream they are married. The woman, Veronica, lies in the first grave. The man, Jeffery, is dying. From his deathbed he instructs us in the details of his burial.

The dream was both understandable and puzzling. In actuality, the two analysts were older, conservative people, strongly committed to upholding conventional relationships between men and women. I was a new analyst, recently divorced, searching for a way to be myself as a woman outside the narrow expectations of traditional culture. The deaths of these two colleagues expressed this transition. My old way of being was indeed dying. This much of the dream I could grasp.

But what were the strange stick figures on the grave and why the palm fronds? I had no idea. Some months later I was startled to find an illustration of similar stick figures in the book *The Great Mother* by Eric Neumann.[2] The text said the looped post was a symbol of the mother goddess and referred the reader to another work, Rachel Levy's *The Gate of Horn*.[3]

Levy's book, which I had to order from England because it was out of print in the United States, explained that the looped post represented the goddess Inanna in Sumerian iconography. Later I found poems to Inanna, which made it clear that palm fronds signified the nourishing date palms gatherers offered to Inanna in her role as goddess of the abundant harvest.

My search at this point was casual. It was the late 1970s. I had never heard of Inanna and knew nothing of her mythology. By chance I then came across several hymns to Inanna in a popular journal, *Parabola*.[4] These hymns from Sumerian sacred marriage texts, translated by Samuel Noah Kramer, glorified Inanna's sexuality and sang praises to her vulva. Suddenly my interest increased quite a lot.

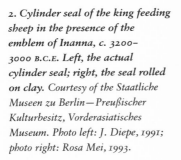

2. Cylinder seal of the king feeding sheep in the presence of the emblem of Inanna, c. 3200– 3000 B.C.E. Left, the actual cylinder seal; right, the seal rolled on clay. Courtesy of the Staatliche Museen zu Berlin — Preußischer Kulturbesitz, Vorderasiatisches Museum. Photo left: J. Diepe, 1991; photo right: Rosa Mei, 1993.

Since Kramer, a renowned Sumerian scholar, had translated most of the hymns and myths about Inanna, I had found a rich resource in his articles and books. The very existence of an ancient body of religious literature that sang praises to a woman's vulva fascinated me. I began to track down the original Sumerian texts. Did the Sumerian language version really say "vulva"? What else might these texts say about women's sexuality? By this time I had a compelling desire to know more of the original language. While the texts were not hard to find in a large university library, they were, of course, in Sumerian. I could not read Sumerian.

This, now twenty years ago, was the beginning of my search for Inanna. Since then she has come to occupy most of my spare time. However, I am getting ahead of the story. For a few years I worked with two graduate students of the Sumerian language at the University of California in Los Angeles. With their help I managed to complete my own renditions of several sacred marriage poems plus the myth "Inanna's Descent to the Underworld." I would take the graduate students' word-for-word translations and develop my own versions.

After a move to northern California, I connected with the department of Near Eastern Studies at the University of California in Berkeley and began to work with Dr. Daniel A. Foxvog, an instructor of Sumerian language and literature. In my long, fruitful relationship with Foxvog, we began with an in-depth study of the sacred marriage texts and the "Descent" myth.

During this repetitive, arduous work I felt myself moving deeper and deeper into the ancient world where Inanna reigned. The work was not

a burden. Rather, the hours with Foxvog were compelling excursions into a strange and distant past. I had no idea what I would do with the poems beyond using Foxvog's explanations to reevaluate the renditions I had already completed. Meanwhile I read everything I could find about ancient Near Eastern civilizations.

A translator at UCLA had told me about a Sumerian poet, Enheduanna, who wrote poems to Inanna. I obtained the book she mentioned, *The Exaltation of Inanna,* which contained a translation of one of these poems.[5] Later, Daniel Foxvog mentioned Enheduanna, saying she had written three poems to Inanna. Together we began to study her work.[6]

Enheduanna was high priestess to the moon god Nanna at his temple at Ur around 2300 B.C.E. Appointed to this sacred position by her father, Sargon of Agade, Enheduanna developed the high priestess's post at Ur, a city in southern Mesopotamia, into the most important religious office in Sumer during the almost forty years she performed her sacred role.

After completing the work with Foxvog, I was left alone with boxes of notes on yellow paper from our study. I chose to work forming the renditions of the poems on my own. I took great pleasure struggling with each line, the sometimes contradictory meanings of a word, the broken sentences, and missing verses. I approached the task as though I were solving a puzzle. I found that slowly the lines would come into focus, and, in the context of the preceding text, I could grasp their apparent meaning.

In the middle of working on the first poem "Inanna and Ebih," I began to get a sense of Enheduanna's love for Inanna. I think it must have been at the point when these beautiful lines became clear:

> Inanna
> child of the Moon God
> a soft bud swelling
> her queen's robe cloaks the slender stem
>
> * * *
>
> steps, yes she steps her narrow foot
> on the furred back
> of a wild lapis lazuli bull
>
> and she goes out
> white-sparked, radiant

in the dark vault of evening's sky
star-steps in the street
through the Gate of Wonder

Enheduanna's love for Inanna became more and more explicit as the translation process progressed. I could feel the real woman who wrote the poems and the vitality of her devotion across the four thousand-year expanse that separates us.

Slowly, the significance of Enheduanna's veneration became apparent. Enheduanna was lifting Inanna out of her established place in Sumerian culture, where she was already considered to be an important goddess, in order to place her above all other deities. Not only was she Enheduanna's personal goddess, but she was now elevated to the supreme position in the Sumerian pantheon.

There is no way to know why Enheduanna made the painstaking effort to elevate Inanna above all the great gods. Perhaps it was simply an act of dedication to her goddess. Still, from this distant point in time, we can conjecture other possibilities.

First, we must get a sense of who Inanna was in the spiritual under-standing of the Sumerians; this is spelled out in Chapter 2. Enheduanna's devotional poems use both metaphor and action to describe Inanna. In these poems we see that the very being of this goddess infuses and vivifies all nature and natural processes. She is the divine in matter. As such, she sustains the ebb and flow, the relentless paradoxical reality of the natural world. She exists between blessing and curse, light and dark, plenty and want, goodness and malevolence, life and death. Harsh as her reality may seem, it is the *Real* every living being must encounter. And she is the *divine* in matter. Implicit in her presence is a divine plan, a sacred order and meaning. Enigmatic as the plan may be, it is inferred by Inanna's careful attention to the workings of the world and the people in it. When Enheduanna elevated Inanna over the other gods, she placed utmost im-portance on this portrayal of the divine presence, the divine infusion into reality.

This belief in the paradoxical nature of reality was not new to the Sumerians, nor to their ancestors, as Chapter 3 explains. Some three millennia before Enheduanna, a Neolithic culture in northern Mesopo-tamia, the Samarran, painted deep plates with vibrant scenes of women with long hair flowing in ecstatic dance, surrounded by a rim of scorpions. The Samarrans also used the ubiquitous, earth-hugging snake symbol in their iconography, as did the later Ubaid culture. The principle Ubaid goddess is a slender snake-headed figure with a high bitumen crown. Often she holds a little snake baby to her breast. Her striking dark crown and human figure suggest both her regal and authoritative nature, as well as her link to humanity. The Neolithic Samarran/Ubaidian lineage continued directly into Sumerian culture.

Enheduanna was "discovered" in the 1920s during Leonard Woolley's archaeological excavations of the city of Ur, to be discussed in Chapter 4. The plaque Woolley found near the residence of the high priestess displayed a carving of Enheduanna in a ritual procession. In writing on the back of the plaque, Enheduanna declares she is dedicating a dais to Inanna in her temple. She identifies herself as "daughter of Sargon." Again, we must ask why Enheduanna would elevate Inanna above all other gods at this particular time? A possible clue lies in the empire-building activities of her father Sargon, examined in Chapter 5. Prior to Sargon, certain kings of various city-states had attained dominant positions in the land. Eannatum of Lagash, for example, around 2500 B.C.E., conquered neighboring cities and even ventured into lands beyond Mesopotamia proper, but he made no attempt to establish a unified government. Sargon was the first leader anywhere to establish an empire, uniting the cities of northern and southern Mesopotamia under his rule and extending his hegemony into neighboring lands far beyond the borders of Sumer and Akkad. As a result of his exploits, he gained enormous prestige over the fifty years of his rule. He had successfully established a new level of central government, something never before achieved. Maintaining and expanding his empire required one military undertaking after another. Living in this new era of empire building and constant military activity must surely have had an effect on the consciousness of the people, who before this had lived in relative peace. Certainly it had an effect on Sargon's daughter Enheduanna.

Sargon, like all the kings before him, invoked the benevolence of Inanna to bring him victory. Sargon equated the Sumerian Inanna with the Akkadian Ishtar, report Hallo and van Dijk, "to lay the theological foundations for a united empire of Sumer and Akkad, and thus ushered in what the chronographic tradition regarded as the 'dynasty of Ishtar.'[7] Although Sargon invoked Inanna in her warrior mode, he expanded Inanna's role as warrior goddess, planting her banner over the new social institution of an established empire. His feats of heroic conquest, previously unmatched in their sustained success and longevity, rode a wave of phallic aggressive energy, new to humanity. The empire Sargon established was perpetuated by his successors, Enheduanna's two brothers and her nephew Naram-Sin, who supported and strengthened this first family dynasty. Naram-Sin even deified himself as the god of Akkad, thus usurping the authority of the powerful priests and priestesses of the temples. It seems possible that Enheduanna elevated the paradoxical Inanna in order to reestablish the balance between the reality of the forces of nature and the hubris of aggressive conquest by an individual human being. Her roles as high priestess and as poet are the subjects of Chapters 6 and 7.

Enheduanna's devotion to Inanna persisted throughout her lifetime. The three poems to Inanna reflect her own spiritual and personal self-integration over time. They document not only the emotional life of this remarkable woman four thousand years ago, but also the personal and spiritual devotion of one woman to her deity, an eloquent diary of adulation and prayer unique in its antiquity. The poems in Part 2 portray what so many women long for, a spirituality grounded in the reflection of a divine woman, offering a full sense of foundation and legitimacy as females. Enheduanna describes a spiritual direction as well, a path for women that encompasses the whole of reality. Inanna's devotees, her "warrior women," "do common work in devotion to you / whose hands sear them with purifying fire." Personal integration based on an embrace of the whole of reality is a searing purification that demands sincere devotion.

A few years ago I found out something else about the symbol of Inanna that had appeared in my dream. Drawn with a stylus on wet clay, the stick figure with the circle on top was her name written in the earliest cuneiform script. You could say she appeared to me as a word, but in that time word and symbol were the same. In the beginning the word "Inanna" was not an abstraction on the page. In the beginning there was not the word but the very presence of the goddess. And there she was in my dream, her stately form planted on the graves of a contemporary couple, a being full of power and mystery waiting to be discovered.

"Great Lady Inanna"

The appearance of Inanna's reed post symbol in my dream raises many questions about the nature of dreams and their personal and cultural meaning. As a Jungian analyst I have studied dream interpretation and worked with hundreds of dream images. I am well aware that numinous images, carrying the most profound meanings, can appear in anyone's dreams.

I first recognized in my dream that the burial scene was related to personal events in my own life. I thought the traditional views of the two analysts being buried indicated that I was being called to let go of certain of my own ties to the values of the collective culture. Inanna's symbol standing tall on the graves was an image of strength and courage from a culture outside of and alien to patriarchal thinking. This new perspective propelled me onto my future path.

Dreams frequently compensate for an excessively one-sided presumption in the dreamer. Inanna was most emphatically a balancing and complementary alternative to the role of mother and homemaker to which I had adapted. But dreams can also carry a larger meaning that pertains to the culture as a whole. Inanna, an important goddess in Sumer for thousands of years, amply balances the one-sidedness of the single male deity of present monotheistic cultures. She is an example of the female element missing in the godhead. Her many-faceted being fills in a vital portion of women's identity.

Inanna's tall reed standards stand like insurgent flags amid the bastion of traditional beliefs that restrict women. I am one of millions of women worldwide who are attempting to redefine themselves and their cultures in ways that foster women's full creative potential. Because my own re-definition seemed, in its essence, to be distilled into this unfamiliar image of a reed post curved into a circle at the top, I felt compelled to know who Inanna was.

My first encounter with Inanna outside my dream found her singing a song to her vulva:

> peg my vulva
> my star-sketched horn of the dipper
> moor my slender boat of heaven
> my new moon crescent cunt beauty[1]
>
> Source: Ni 9602, obverse, column 1, my translation

I followed this lead and found the courtship and love songs of a sacred marriage ritual that described a goddess of unbridled sexuality actively pursuing the object of her desire. While these images go against the mod-esty and decorum most patriarchal societies idealize in women, they are not beyond the fantasy or experience of most women. The idea of Inanna's audacious lust being part of a sacred canon triggered delight-ful thoughts of inserting these poems between the pages of Bible stories taught in the stony church of my childhood. This Inanna was a personage I could wholeheartedly embrace.

The many sides of Inanna's sexuality captivated me for some time, but hints of her darker aspects also began to emerge as I read. The whole vision of this goddess was beyond anything I had ever imagined. My con-tinuing investigation of the dream image lifted me off familiar ground and set me down in a strange landscape. In the myth "Inanna's Descent to the Underworld," Inanna is stripped, beaten, killed, hung on a peg to rot, miraculously revived, and returned to earth transformed. In that myth I met an Inanna who brought back from the great below the very eye of death. But it was not until I read Enheduanna's poems to Inanna that I began to see the full extent of her being. Enheduanna's Inanna is a paradoxical creature that mirrors a wide range of characteristics all the way from the most horrendous, vicious, cruel, destructive, and violent to the most beneficent, glorious, and creative. In her poetry Enheduanna captured a vision of a larger, wider, deeper self called Inanna, and in that vision she found a reflection of the immensity of the imagination beyond the personal ego, and far beyond cultural traditions. Inanna is an archetypal image of profound significance that constellated itself in human consciousness six thousand years ago and now returns to us offering her excruciating, dreadful, magnificent picture of the way things are.

More than any other goddess or god in the Sumerian pantheon, Inanna embodies the totality of "What Is." In that regard she represents the attempt of the Sumerian psyche to contain and to organize their apprehension of the chaotic, indecipherable, ineffable mystery of the known and the unknown universe. She is their version of a personification of the whole of reality.

The Reed Posts

The graceful image of the tall reed posts with the head-like circle at the top appears on numerous clay tablets, cylinder seals, carvings, and religious articles from prehistoric Mesopotamia in the late fourth millennium.[2] A flowing "ribbon" falls from the head in many examples and resembles a woman's long hair. Archaeologist Beatrice Laura Goff calls it "the beribboned standard."[3] The earliest writing of cuneiform on clay tablets is found at Uruk.[4] Inanna's sign appears on these tablets accompanied by a star, the element that designates divinity. This is the first known written record of Inanna's name. The frequency of Inanna's sign, **mùš**,[5] on the archaic tablets from Uruk substantiates the importance, if not the primacy, of her cult there. Symbols of other gods rarely appear on these tablets.[6]

By careful study of these early tablets from Uruk, Krystyna Szarzynska

3. Early pictographic signs for the goddess Inanna. From Archaische Texte aus Uruk *by A. Falkenstein (Berlin, Deutsche Forschungsgemeinschaft, 1936), Zeishenliste, fig. 208.*

(a)   (b)   (c)

4. Early signs from Uruk tablets: (a) "Princely Inanna"; (b) "Morning Inanna"; (c) "Evening Inanna." Author's drawings from Szarzynska, 1993.

found that in this period Inanna had four separate aspects, three of which received particular offerings. She was worshiped as "Princely Inanna" [ᵈInanna-nun], "Morning Inanna" [ᵈInanna-ud/húd], and "Evening Inanna" [ᵈInanna-sig]. No offering tablets have been found for her fourth form, Inanna of the Steppe [ᵈInanna-kur].[7] "Morning" and "Evening" Inanna refer to Inanna's identification as the morning and evening star we call Venus.

Although many of the signs on the tablets that designate particular offerings cannot be deciphered, some can be understood. "Princely Inanna" received various types of grains and breads, beer, dairy products, sheep, and swine. "Morning Inanna" received sheep, silver, foodstuffs, grain, and certain items cooked with flour. "Evening Inanna" received grain products, flour, wool, carpenter's tools, and other raw materials. The offering registers for "Morning" and "Evening" Inanna were signed by individuals with well-known official titles, meaning that record keeping of offerings even at this early time was an important aspect of the worship of Inanna. Although the offerings to the three aspects of Inanna overlap somewhat, their differences remain consistent.[8]

While the numerous examples of Inanna's symbol on the Uruk tablets strengthen our understanding of her importance, the extensive archaeological excavations of Uruk, the principal center of her worship, provide more contextual information. In the late fourth millennium, Uruk was the largest, most important city in Mesopotamia. At its center was the Eanna, a cluster of large buildings that Hans Nissen describes as:

the very large economic unit . . . that controlled not only agriculture, animal husbandry, and the crafts, but also trade. . . . Clearly, it was also responsible for the

5. *Votive plaque from the* gipar *at Ur, Early Dynastic III period, c. 2500 B.C.E. Inanna's ring-post symbol stands on either side of the doorway into the temple. Note the front-facing figure with rolled-brim hat in the lower register, the hat typical of that worn by the high priestess.* Courtesy of the Trustees of The British Museum, BM 118561.

building and maintenance of the temple complex as well as for the organization of religious festivals and the supervision of sacrifices.[9]

Inanna's temple dominated the Eanna throughout the history of Uruk. Certain Sumerian scholars see this symbol of Inanna as a gatepost situated on either side of the doorway to the storehouse. A rolled mat, hung between the two posts, could be pulled down to form a door. Nissen describes them as "two so-called reed-ring bundles, the original doorposts in the traditional reed architecture of the country: the loops on either side of the door opening hang the poles around which the rush mats that served as door curtains were wound."[10] This symbol, then, signified Inanna's position as guardian of the abundant harvest kept in the communal storehouse. As a doorpost, Inanna guards the passageway between two worlds, the outside ordinary world and the inside sacred womb-shaped sanctuary that shelters the abundant harvest.

Inanna's emblem was made from the ubiquitous reeds that grow in the delta region at the confluence of the Tigris and Euphrates rivers. Even in present-day Iraq, houses in the delta are constructed of reeds. The emblem that signified her presence was made of the common building material that fills the marshlands, that liminal space separating the river waters and dry land. The doorway to the storehouse marked the transitional space between secular outside and hallowed inside. In her most elemental form, "the beribboned standard" heralded the entrance into that special state of mind called the sacred.

Inanna's Mythology

The origin of the Sumerian people remains a contested issue (see Chapter 3), but a number of hypotheses have been proposed concerning antecedents of Sumerian mythology based on iconography. Sumerian scholar J. van Dijk traces certain Sumerian mythologems back to ancient shamanistic practices, saying, "an interdependence seems to be undeniable." [11] He contends that the gathering of these mythological elements took place in an ancient period of human history, and that we are therefore unable to reconstruct the process of their dispersal.[12] "One could make a long list of mythic motifs," he says, "that the country of Sumer has in common with other people." [13] The incorporation of motifs from other mythologies is a prime example of the Sumerian propensity to embellish their culture with elements assimilated from other ethnic groups.

While Inanna has a particularly Sumerian quality, she also absorbed characteristics and mythologems from the distant prehistoric past. Enheduanna intimates Inanna's connection to her ancestors in these lines:

> you wear the robes
> of the old, old gods

Certain words in the Sumerian language suggest that the Sumerians came to the Mesopotamian plains from a mountain region—some scholars pinpoint the Iranian plateau. Enheduanna keeps the mountain tradition alive when she calls Inanna "mountain born." Inanna, and her Semitic counterpart Ishtar, is goddess of the planet Venus in both its morning and evening aspects, as we have seen from the archaic Uruk tablets. She is the daughter of the moon couple Nanna and Ningal, and thus is a third-generation goddess, granddaughter of Enlil and Ninlil, and great-granddaughter of the original gods An [Heaven] and Ki [Earth]. An and Ki were united on the cosmic mountain that was born out of the primordial sea. This cosmic mountain is reflected in the Sumerian temple structure: the holy sanctuary of the ziggurat stands on the top of a terraced "mountain."

A recounting of the Sumerian creation myth occurs in the tale "Gilgamesh, Enkidu, and the Nether World." Van Dijk cites the relationship between one section of this myth, "Inanna and the Huluppu-tree," with the shamanistic world-tree motif known in many parts of the ancient world.[14] In his study of Assyrian prophecies of Ishtar dating from the seventh century B.C.E., Simo Parpola connects the central symbol of Judaism, the menorah, to the ancient Near Eastern sacred tree, saying "the entire associated doctrinal apparatus" of the Judaic Tree of Life "can be shown to be based on a Mesopotamian model perfected in Assyria in the second millennium B.C.E."[15] It is possible that Inanna's reed post symbol, first evident in the third millennium B.C.E., derives from the mythologem of the world tree or from the celestial pole that connects heaven and earth, the symbol of the ultimate point of orientation.[16] We can think of Inanna, with her complex mix of characteristics, as an attempt to bring together the seemingly chaotic forces of the universe into one unifying, and therefore orienting, personification.

Modern tradition places the beginning of philosophy with the pre-Socratics "who were able to conceptualize unity within the universe."[17] Piotr Michalowski challenges this late origin, using as evidence "the structural and symbolic patterns through which the Mesopotamians expressed their search for meaning in the universe."[18] Enheduanna reveres Inanna herself as the unifying god-image saying, "she wears the carved-out ground plan / of heaven and earth." Having evolved from the Sumerian Inanna, the Assyrian Ishtar is an aspect of the unified god, says Parpola, who develops a case for "the basic similarity of the Assyrian and biblical concepts of God."[19] The first written evidence of this intriguing developmental line comes in Enheduanna's insistence that Inanna is "greater than the great gods" and that she is the supreme expression of the unity in the plurality of the universe.

On the one hand, Inanna consolidates themes from ancient religious practices. On the other hand, she is thoroughly Mesopotamian and unique. Unlike any other Sumerian deity, Inanna, like a magnet, attracted a multitude of powers that, as she says in Enheduanna's poetry, "gave my word weight above all others." I try to imagine how the nature of this force called Inanna swept the religious consciousness of the Mesopotamians into its vortex, sucking away powers from even the most prominent gods of the pantheon. Inanna is an irresistible directional movement of the imagination. We have nothing in the western pantheons of goddesses that even approaches her variety and dominion. Inanna is a unique outbreak of a particular consciousness attempting to embody and define itself. She is an expression of the Mesopotamian psyche that manifested itself in this paradoxical, complex, divine woman.

Time after time in Mesopotamian myth and poetry, Inanna gains more powers, the **me** (pronounced "may"). According to Mark Hall, the meaning of the word "is loosely rendered as 'power' but has such a wide range of connotations and applications as to defy any precise definition of its meaning." [20] In the myth of "Inanna and Enki: the Transfer of the Arts of Civilization from Eridu to Erech," Inanna tricks a drunken Enki into giving her his **me**, those principles of order over which the Sumerian gods preside. She successfully escapes to her own port with all that Enki has given her. In the myth of "Inanna's Descent to the Underworld," she dares to sit on the throne of her sister, Queen of the Underworld Ereshkigal, and returns with underworld powers. In Enheduanna's poetry, Inanna is raised above all other gods, who bend and quiver in her presence. In a late composition, "The Elevation of Inanna," the great god of heaven, An, marries Inanna as the council of gods has proposed, gives her his name and his powers. Enlil then gives her his powers and Enki follows suit. Inanna becomes virtual Queen of the Universe.

W. W. Hallo says "the attribution to Inanna of these **me**'s represents the main point of both of Enheduanna's hymns" ("Lady of Largest Heart" and "The Exaltation of Inanna") and that Inanna's "preoccupation with the **me**'s may almost be said to approach the character of an obsession in Sumerian literature." [21] If we treat this "obsession" as a directional force in the Mesopotamian psyche, an idea is striving to be born that finds its embodiment in an Inanna who reaches toward being the one all-powerful deity. The Sumerian characterization of Inanna emerges as an all-encompassing, over-arching deity, even an attempt at a unitary vision. In his discussion of Assyrian prophecies, Parpola urges that we not see polytheism and monotheism as mutually exclusive. He argues that the Assyrian Ishtar, the Semitic Inanna, is an aspect of the god Aššur . . .

"she, however, is at the same time also an entity *distinct* from Aššur: a divine power working in man and thus bridging the gulf between man and god." [22] In Parpola's interesting thesis, Inanna/Ishtar is comparable to the Holy Spirit, the aspect of the one God that manifests in relation to humans.

Inanna was a goddess who attracted the powers not only of the known world but those of the entire cosmos, "the carved out ground plan / of heaven and earth." She embraced the full continuum of authority from the darkest to the most brilliant. A creature of earth as well as heaven, she reflected paradoxical human nature. It is to her characteristic display of paradox that we now turn.

The Paradoxical Goddess

Many creation myths begin with a swirling fog that gives no hint of the myriad possibilities of a differentiated world. In the beginning, as the myths often say, there is a unity that divides into its countless parts. Jung says of this original unity:

(The *unus mundus*) as we have seen (is) the potential world of the first day of creation, when nothing was yet "in actu," i.e., divided into two and many but was still one. [23]

In Mesopotamian mythology this unity is the primeval sea, Nammu, that gives birth to the cosmic mountain, already containing a united An and Ki, heaven and earth. [24] Creation divides the original oneness into pairs of opposites, above/below, day/night, and these pairs of linked opposites are called a syzygy. "God unfolds himself in the world in the form of syzygies (paired opposites), such as heaven/earth, day/night, male/female, etc.," Jung says. [25] Unlike the pair An and Ki, (heaven and earth, male and female), Inanna is a single deity in whose being the opposing pairs of creation are gathered.

Humans reflect this characteristic of Inanna. The infant in its primordial sea slowly begins to differentiate between states of being: hunger, satiation; pain, comfort. The natural process of development involves becoming aware of paradoxical opposites. As adults we recognize our own dualities: love/hate, generosity/stinginess, compassion/indifference. Psychological growth involves a continuing confrontation with the shadowy motives and elements that lie beneath the surface of our public presentation of ourselves. This process is central to our understanding of Inanna, and we will meet it throughout this book.

Inanna was the only Mesopotamian deity whose character so prominently included contradictions. This characteristic reflected a central Mesopotamian perspective, one that Assyriologist Rivkah Harris depicts as, "the existence of antitheses and contradictions, the delicate balancing of order and disorder," [26] "a deity who incorporated fundamental and irreducible paradoxes." [27] In her actions, Inanna exhibits both benevolent light and threatening dark. Her violence and destructiveness go beyond the boundaries of tolerable human behavior. She carries light and dark to their extremes. Inanna's immense popularity in antiquity must be related in part to the fact that she could reflect not only the best in human nature, but she could also exhibit what is abhorrent, unpleasant, dirty, sinful, terrifying, abnormal, perverse, obsessive, murderous, mad, and violent.

All of Inanna's menacing characteristics appear in Enheduanna's poetry. Inanna is a lioness "prowling the roads / shows wet fangs / gnashes her teeth." An eagle, "her fiendish wings flap in foreign lands." We know Inanna was a war goddess; kings carried her emblem into battle. "Woe the city under her frown," says the poet. Her glance caused crops to wither, cattle to perish. She loves battle, but her "fiendish wings" soar over her own people as well, leaving destruction in their wake. "The wide stall of animals / she mauls / slashes the cows and bulls." Her floods "swamp the one she loathes." She is a "pit trap for the headstrong." The evil and proud bend under her weight.

Inanna is a mirror of what Jung called "the abysmal contradictions of human nature." [28] She shows us our oppositions in sharp relief. She is a divine manifestation of the ultimate conjunction of opposites, displaying for humankind its contradictory nature.

Wholeheartedly a goddess of war and destruction, she is equally a goddess of love. Kings claim her as their bride and unite with her in the sacred marriage ritual. For Dumuzi, her spouse, she says:

> Listen
> I will scrub my skin with soap
> I will dry myself with linen
> I will put on mighty love clothes

> I know how exactly
> I will look so fine
> I will make you feel like a king
> *Source: Ni 9602, obverse, column 1, my trans.*

She sings to him, "vulva moist in the flood lands / the queen asks who brings the ox." Joan Goodnick Westenholz describes Sumerian love songs:

Passionate love and sexual yearnings for the beloved characterize almost all the songs. Moreover, the marriage theme permeates the poetry; the bridal sheets, laid out on a marriage bed, are where the consummation of love is to take place. Jerrold S. Cooper has claimed that Sumerian love poetry expressed female sexuality, that it "privileges the female organ over the male," whereas Sumerian narrative poetry praised male sexuality.[29]

Inanna is goddess of love, but no one owns her. She "goes about" as a prostitute. She is the goddess of prostitutes. She waits in the tavern. Enheduanna entices her, saying, "I have readied your room in the tavern," the domain of prostitutes. Nevertheless, she watches over marriage: "to have a husband / to have a wife / to thrive in the goodness of love / are yours Inanna." It is likewise hers "to build a house," "to kiss a baby's lips." Inanna presides over all facets of love. Westenholz confirms saying, "The passion for love as well as the joy its consummation achieved were deemed attributes of Inanna. . . . Accordingly, any manifestation of love betrayed her presence and activity."[30]

This goddess is not bound by being female. She appropriates maleness and strides in the male domain. She is a warrior. She darts forth in battle. She dresses in androgynous power garments, a queen's robe, a carnelian necklace, fire beams painted on her forehead, a seven-headed mace in her fist. She even turns man into woman, woman into man. She embraces androgyny "inventing," the poet says, the head overturning ritual that takes a woman, gives her a male emblem of power, a mace, and ritually anoints her an ecstatic priestess. This priestess joins other of Inanna's temple personnel whose sexuality blurs gender boundaries.

Inanna's cultic celebrations were wild and playful affairs filled with songs and dance. They were occasions to mock social order. They were carnivals that encouraged outrageous conduct. S. N. Kramer suggests

these celebrations were connected to the sacred marriage rite, "one of
the principal components of Inanna's cult . . . characterized by orgiastic,
ecstatic behavior, and probably even by bloody castration, on the part of
some of its participants."[31]

For among these we find male prostitutes with special beribboned hairdos; hiero-
dules of various categories; men and woman carrying sword-belts and spears;
devotees who dressed their right side in women's clothing and their left side in
men's clothing; dagger-holding *kurgarras;* worshipers who kept sprinkling blood
from their blood-covered daggers—to mention only those whose function and
behavior are intelligible to some extent.[32]

On the cosmic level, Inanna pulls the rug out from under our belief
in order and principle. She is the element of chaos that hangs over every
situation, the reminder that cultures and rules and traditions and order
are constructs of humanity. Society congeals possibility into laws and
mores so that we can live together. Inanna reminds us these are but prod-
ucts of the mind. At bottom all is possible.

Inanna feeds the creative spirit that stretches the imagination beyond
social confines. She is a goddess unbound by social order. She is the un-
thinkable thought, a constant reminder that what seems pinned down,
fixed, certain, is not. She confronts us with the unbearable uncertainty
that form and structure are merely "as if" solid and secure.

While Inanna's polarities and contradictions generate creativity, they
also provoke insecurity, disruption, and terror. Social disorder can be
violent and destructive. Primitive rivalries and genocide can erupt in
the most advanced societies. Sexual freedom and the blurring of gender
boundaries can rouse the hatred of those whose beliefs are threatened.

The Mesopotamians had the wisdom to keep a foot in both worlds.
On one side was the traditionally defined Mesopotamian culture. On the
other was infinite cosmic potentiality held before their eyes in the form
of the goddess Inanna. Structure and security bordered destruction and
chaos. The other gods and goddesses, and even Inanna, upheld the prin-
ciples of an orderly society. But Inanna also epitomized the essence of
contradiction, of the unimaginable variety and possibility in the created
world. These two sides were kept alive in the myth and ritual of the god-
dess Inanna.

The profound meaning embodied in Inanna developed historically in

the fourth millennium alongside an increasingly male-dominated gov-
ernment, economic, and social order. The rule of kings tended toward an
authoritarianism that demanded citizens obey hierarchical class struc-
tures and mores. Pressure was applied to extract conformity. Against this
template of the good citizen, Inanna introduced cosmic disorder and dis-
obedience. She introduced the possibility of the individual who thinks
for herself/himself.

Inanna confronts us with ourselves. The question of choices, of how
to live one's life, is always present. Conflict and contradiction confront
us daily. To take Inanna seriously is to face the expansiveness of our own
freedom. Through the choices we make, we build the unique individu-
ality of ourselves.

Inanna's presence draws us into the realm of the inner life. She is the
guide who insists we face our shadowy contradictions, that we own who
we really are in all our painful and wonderful complexity. As the goddess
of paradox, she is the model of unity in multiplicity. Each of us reflects
a bit of her discordance in ourselves. Each of us is burdened with the
chore of gathering our many conflicting pieces together into a semblance
of order and congruence. Enheduanna first understood the challenge of
living in devotion to Inanna.

CHAPTER

3

˄ ˅

"The Robes of the
Old, Old Gods"

The goddess Inanna is an expression of an ancient spiritual belief that the gods and goddesses reside in the infinite forms of the material world around us. This principle of the immanence of the divine in matter appears to be the underlying religious conviction of Paleolithic and Neolithic cultures in Europe and the ancient Near East. Because there was no writing in these earlier periods, we can only deduce the beliefs from the artifacts that remain. There is a preponderance of visual evidence that, as in Bronze Age Mesopotamia, these ancient religions revolved around ritual worship of the divine process as it unfolded in the natural world.

Enheduanna's poetry provides a vivid description of the worship of a goddess who is immanent in nature. Her writing is a treasure of ideas and practices that likely show traces of very ancient beliefs. As I began to grasp Inanna's multifaceted character, I wanted to know if she inherited her paradoxical nature from some ancient ancestress. I looked to Mesopotamian prehistory for the answers. The first evidence of religious practice in Mesopotamia comes from the bones of the Neanderthal. Four skeletons lay buried in Shanidar Cave in the Zagros Mountains that span Iraq's eastern boundary. The burial dates from 50,000 B.C.E.[1] Archaeologist Ralph Solecki found fossil pollen at Shanidar, evidence that their Neanderthal kin brought rare flowers from many miles away to scatter on the bodies of the dead.[2]

Later, Upper Paleolithic settlements of *Homo sapiens* are evident in Iraqi Kurdistan. These first inhabitants of the ancient Near East lived in

23

caves or temporary camps. In northern Iraq around 10,000 B.C.E., near Shanidar Cave, which had been inhabited by their Neanderthal ancestors, a group practiced a ritual that included the wearing of goat heads and the wings of the white-tailed sea eagle. Such scenes were found depicted in the much later (5600 B.C.E.) culture of Çatal Hüyük in central Turkey, a settlement on the trade routes of the early Mesopotamians.[3] Painted on the walls of shrines at Çatal Hüyük are human figures with feathered wings on their arms. This motif appears to be a human imitation of the deity as a great bird. Inanna, in Enheduanna's poetry, flies over her domain as a bird, repeating this ancient practice. The similarities in these ritual images, separated in time and location, may be only a coincidence inherent in the range of images that can express certain spiritual beliefs, or they may indicate the continuity of a widespread, common story as J. J. van Dijk suggests (see Chapter 2).

The sea-eagle priests lived during the transition between the Upper Paleolithic and the Neolithic eras. In Mesopotamia this progression into the self-sufficient villages of the Neolithic took place slowly over thousands of years, in the canyons, piedmont terraces, and plains of the great arc of the Zagros Mountains on Iraq's eastern border. Charles Keith Maisels has traced this development step-by-step and describes " 'settling down' along the Zagrosian Arc" as "a long drawn-out process of reduction in mobility by steps, until year-round settlement arrived."[4] Using the work of Joan Oates,[5] Maisels describes three phases of this transition. The first, 9000 to 7000 B.C.E., is characterized by intensified food gathering in a broad-spectrum economy.

A typical site in the second phase, 7000 to 6000 B.C.E., is that of Jarmo, in a montane valley south of the cave at Shanidar. Jarmo was an early village farming community, still dependent on gathering and hunting that lasted possibly three hundred years. Archaeologists found thousands of clay figurines at Jarmo, both animal and human. Many of the small, crudely sculpted female figurines from 6750 B.C.E. sit on heavy thighs. This goddess is immense, slow moving, and weighs down the earth's surface. Her bulk is reminiscent of the earlier thirty thousand-year-old female figurines found from Spain to Russia. The continuity of this tradition seems to be an expression of the belief in the immanence of the divine. The ample goddess can represent the sheer weight of matter that binds humanity to the earth.

Three cultures that overlap chronologically and geographically represent phase three of the transition from the Paleolithic period to Neolithic

6. Female figurine from Jarmo. *Courtesy of the Oriental Institute of the University of Chicago.*

villages in Mesopotamia. Beginning about 6000 B.C.E., the Hassuna, Samarra, and Halaf "constitute the earliest distinct agricultural *cultures* anywhere."[6] These three represent, according to Maisels, "the developed village community, the epitome of the Neolithic 'revolution.'"[7] The earliest Hassuna settlements on virgin soil are the first on the Meso-

potamian plain and appear to be confined to northern Iraq. From a Has-
suna burial we know that priestesses directed some portions of Hassuna
worship. A woman's body, painted with red ocher, was found adorned
with beads and shells, a style of burial repeated in other cultures only
for a few women. The consistent architecture that developed among the
Hassuna seemed to accommodate one large family. These houses formed
the primary living arrangement throughout the culture.

In significant contrast, the dwelling unit of the Samarran culture, that
began shortly after the Hassuna, was not the nuclear family but an ex-
tended family including, eventually, workers, servants, and retainers, all
living in large T-form structures. This core social unit, larger than a kin-
ship unit, is especially meaningful because it prevailed throughout the
Samarran period, into the subsequent Ubaid culture and the following
Uruk period that led to historical Sumer. The "augmented households
structured around a dominant family," Maisels asserts, evolved from
"the demands imposed by the concentration of resources and storage
where rainfed agriculture is not viable or highly risky." [8] Significantly,
at the Samarran site of Tell Es-Sawwan on the east bank of the Tigris,
called by Joan Oates "the most important prehistoric site that has been
excavated in Iraq," [9] small ditches for irrigation were uncovered along
the edge of the site, marking the beginning of the evolution of irrigation
subsistence. The development of irrigation and the household living pat-
tern and architecture that supported an irrigation economy began at this
early date and continued into the Sargonic period and Enheduanna's life-
time. As we will see later, this "great household," or **é-gal**, with its food
storage capacity, became the model for the Sumerian temple.

The community at Sawwan developed other elements that continued
into the Sumerian culture: stamp seals that could be pressed into wet clay
as well as mud-bricks cast in molds, a process that Sumerians eventually
used in their architecture. Joan Oates connects the female figurines from
the Samarran site at Sawwan to the later "lizard-headed figurines" of the
Ubaid. A figure of a male found at Sawwan is one of the few discovered in
Mesopotamian prehistoric sites. Oates says, "Male figurines are rare in
Mesopotamia. No other complete example is known until the end of the
'Ubaid period, and they are equally rare in Anatolia and Iran." [10] Maisels
suggests the unusual " 'coffee-bean' eyes" of the Samarran goddess could
represent the seeds of dates that later pertained to Inanna in Sumer, god-
dess of the date storehouse. [11] Sumerian culture in these respects may be
indebted to the sixth millennium Neolithic Samarrans.

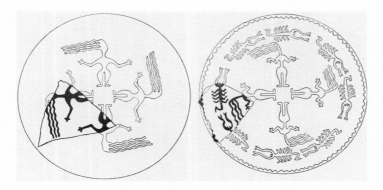

7. *Samarran deep plates with scorpions and long-haired female figures. Courtesy of Yale University Press.*

The Samarrans painted large deep plates with striking, dynamic designs of female and animal figures. Women with flowing hair, fishes, birds, deer, and scorpions vibrate in circular movement around the center. Rows of dancing women ring the borders. Energetic motion shimmers in these scenes, barely contained by the plate's rim. Scorpion and goddess are held together in some ancient meaning, juxtaposing the hair-flowing goddess and her deadly sting, the ecstasy of her energetic joy beside the venomous sting of fate. This paradoxical alignment recurs thousands of years later in the goddess Inanna who continued to be associated with the scorpion, particularly in the form of Ishara, the goddess Ishtar/Inanna as mother.[12]

The Halaf culture, appearing some five hundred to eight hundred years after the inception of the Hassuna and Samarra, began in the far north of Iraq, but by its middle phase it had spread southward. Eventually, its well-integrated settlements reached from the Mediterranean to the eastern boundaries of Iraq and beyond.[13] It was a highly evolved culture of agricultural villages. The Halaf developed pottery with a beauty and variety unknown to this point. Its designs are at times exquisitely intricate abstract forms, at other times repeated realistic depictions of birds, giraffes, bulls or bucrania, or snakes coiled, ready to strike. On one pot a graceful heron spreads its wings between the borders as it flies in a field of stars. The Halaf produced hundreds of goddess figurines. She continues to sit on her great thighs as in Jarmo. Often her arms bend in a graceful curve around her ample breasts. Her body may be painted with

8. Halaf period female figure, possibly a goddess, from Tchargar Bazar. Courtesy of the Trustees of the British Museum, BM 125318.

red stripes. She may wear a painted necklace or a striking V on her chest, reminiscent of the goddesses of Old Europe excavated by Marija Gimbutas.[14] Sometimes she has a large eye painted on her stubby head, eyelashes or rays above and below, giving her a startled and all-seeing appearance. The great eye continues to appear on the goddesses of Sumer, and became the dominant cult image at the northern eye temple at Tell Brak in the Uruk period, imagery that was strongly connected to Inanna's worship in the south.

With the succeeding culture, the Ubaidians, around 5000 B.C.E., we enter a familiar society, whose continuity, from the Ubaid period onward, is "beyond question" according to Robert Adams.[15] It became the most widespread of the Neolithic cultures in the north and south of

Mesopotamia, reaching even into eastern Saudi Arabia. It occupied the same northern sites as the Halaf, superseding that culture. Archaeologist Seton Lloyd says of the Ubaidians, "These were the Sumerians." [16] Maisels goes further, saying the Ubaid "derives from the Samarran and ultimately supplants the Halaf culture tradition," [17] thus tracing Sumerian cultural continuity back another thousand years. In the south, the Ubaidians established the principal Sumerian cities of Eridu, Ur, Uruk, and al-'Ubaid.

The origin of the Sumerians continues to be a subject of considerable debate. Some scholars believe the Sumerians migrated from the Iranian Plateau region long ago. Archaeologist Joan Oates says, "Although we cannot deny the possibility of an Iranian origin for the Mesopotamian cultures in question, there is certainly no positive evidence to support this hypothesis." [18] She makes a convincing case for the continuity of the culture from Ubaid times onward, citing a number of ongoing temple features including the architectural arrangements of the rooms, location of ritual burning, the decoration of the facade, libation vessels, certain offerings, and the symbol of the snake. When in her poetry Enheduanna uses images such as "the first snake," or "mistress eagle," or describes Inanna as a great bird circling the sky, or juxtaposes Inanna's terrible contradictions, we hear echoes of an ancient tradition that reaches back into the Neolithic.

Perhaps the most striking evidence of continuity is at the southern city of Eridu where eighteen temples were built one on top of the other over thousands of years, a sign of the builders' desire to preserve a connection to the common religious beliefs of the past. The first temple, a small room resting on clean sand built around 5000 B.C.E., has the standard features of later Mesopotamian temples: a niche, two platforms, an altar, and offering table. An oven stood outside this room. Eridu was the temple home of Enki, god of wisdom and sweet waters. The remains of fish sacrifice suggest he was worshiped in the earliest temples. Oates says of Eridu, "It is extremely difficult to believe that the location of the temple, its cult, and even its architecture would have continued in an unbroken tradition from al-'Ubaid to Sumerian times if there had been during this period any major change in the character of the population." [19]

A slender goddess figurine with reptilian head contrasts strikingly with the earlier ample figures. In examples from Ur, Uruk, and Eridu, she wears a conical headdress or crown of bitumen; her snake eyes slant,

9. Snake-headed figure of a woman holding a child, al-Ubaid period. Courtesy of the Iraq Museum, Baghdad.

barely open between puffy lids. On her exaggerated shoulders are raised discs. These are keloid scars, an excessive growth of scar tissue thought by many cultures to indicate extraordinary powers.[20] Her pubic triangle is drawn with rays or lines. Frequently she holds a snake-headed baby to her small breasts. We are reminded of Enheduanna's poem that has Inanna say, "like the FIRST SNAKE / coming out of the mountain."

In the last five hundred years of the Ubaid period a temple was constructed in the city of Uruk at the site of Inanna's temple, the Eanna. In a successor temple, from the ensuing Uruk period, Inanna's cuneiform sign first made its appearance on several tablets. The sign appears again on a beautiful alabaster vase whose carving tells a myth of a bearded man bringing gifts to the door of the goddess, probably an early representation of the sacred marriage ritual. Henri Frankfort calls this vase "one of the most important monuments of the 'Proto-literate' period."[21]

Inanna's tall reed posts also emerge from an apparent reed hut carved on a trough found in the Eanna district. Frankfort says, "This building is probably either an archaic type of shrine or the fold of the flock of Inanna."[22]

10. The Warka vase (Uruk, 3000 B.C.E.) with a scene of offerings being presented to the goddess Inanna. Courtesy of the Iraq Museum, Baghdad.

In the Uruk period, beginning around 4000 B.C.E., the Sumerian culture experienced a creative renaissance. This burst is apparent in the fourth millennium with the expansion of writing on clay tablets and the proliferation of cylinder seals. The renaissance is also evident in temple architecture, in the spread of the culture, and in the vast increase in the population. This is the time of the first city-states. The major population centers were at Uruk and in the Nippur area. In these large centers, a significant number of people were freed of the need to work in food production, and were therefore able to devote themselves to arts and crafts. Nissen concludes "that in the period of early high civilization communal energies were evidently released to such an extent that speedy and comprehensive changes took place in all fields of life"[23] Rudimentary writing began with "lists of gods, professions, geographic names, and classes of objects arranged in conceptual categories."[24] The fourth millennium experienced relative peacefulness. In the ages before and through the fourth millennium, wars and skirmishes occurred, but they were not the

overwhelming center of life that they later became in the third millennium.[25]

In her book *Before Writing*, Denise Schmandt-Besserat traces the origin of cuneiform script to the variety of shapes of clay tokens used for counting found in Mesopotamian Neolithic sites from 8000 B.C.E. onward.[26] The first pictographic characters on clay tablets that have been discovered came from levels dating to 3300 B.C.E. in the Inanna temple at Uruk. These tablets contain some seven hundred signs, the number demonstrating that the written word was already well established. Even so, it took another seven hundred years before cuneiform script developed sufficiently to produce texts that can be described as literature. Enheduanna lived a thousand years after the Uruk texts were produced.

During the course of this thousand years, the expanding Sumerian society began to call its rulers kings, developed governing bodies for cities, armed its city-states, built city walls for protection, and centered its growing commerce in the temples. The offices of priest and priestess evolved into important positions at the heart of each city. In this, the Early Dynastic period, 2960–2360 B.C.E., new urban institutions developed, creating new positions of power. While scattered rural communities were prevalent during the preceding Jemdet Nasr period, this population pattern changed as people migrated to the cities. Possibly, the large temples, their cultic practices, and their opportunities for employment drew people from the rural areas. In addition, the growing shortage of water meant that food production was limited to areas near the irrigation canals. The temples became important centers for food distribution and formed the social and religious core of the cities.

11. *Alabaster trough from Warka (Uruk), Jemdet Nasr period. Opposite page, end view; above, side view. Inanna's reed-post symbol figures prominently with the herd and the storehouse. Courtesy of the Trustees of the British Museum, BM 120000.*

The title **en**, used to refer to the high priestess or priest, appeared by the end of the fourth millennium or beginning of the third in the Jemdet Nasr period. This designation's appearance precedes that for king, **lugal**, by a thousand years, emphasizing the preeminence the institution of the temple had over the political office of the king.

The first Early Dynastic (ED) period ended in 2760 B.C.E. with a great flood that has been memorialized in the Gilgamesh epic, a flood which was, according to Max Mallowan, "transmitted, perhaps through Canaanite mythology, to the Old Testament record."[27] From this time forward the water supply receded, and, according to Nissen, this "can broadly be regarded as the cause of a qualitative change in ways of political coexistence."[28] The regional conflicts sought to settle disputes over water and other resources.

A series of temples to Inanna has been discovered in Nippur, a city that became the most important religious center in Mesopotamia. Mallowan suggests that the ED II temple to Inanna "may have originated from an earlier, prehistoric foundation."[29] The temple was large, 275 feet long and 85 feet wide, an indication of its importance. Quite possibly the ritual crowning of the king at Nippur by Inanna began as early as the Early Dynastic period.

Social stratification began with the property ownership of the large households, the é-**gal**, originating in Samarran times. Male descendants of the chief men of the household inherited property. Patrilineal legacy, well established in the Early Dynastic period, may have been implicit in the fifth millennium Samarran household organization. The heads of the 'great houses' formed a council of elders who ran the cities alongside an

12. Jemdet Nasr period tablet, c. 3000 B.C.E. Possibly a list of offerings with the first sign in each of the first three rows the rising sun, indicating day one, day two, day three. Courtesy of the Trustees of the British Museum, BM 116730.

assembly of male citizens. The first definite reference to the **lugal**, king, occurred in 2700 B.C.E. at the city of Kish, by which time evidence shows there was a royal palace. The king was chosen from the council of elders, and therefore was a functionary of the cities, not a powerful man around whom the city populations gathered. These great households were economic units as well as living units. Significantly, by Sargonic times, the level of literacy in most large households was high. Every such household included "at least one person able to read, write, and calculate."[30]

During the six hundred years of the ED period only fourteen major cities existed in Mesopotamia. Each was essentially a self-sufficient city-state. Military skirmishes occurred between neighboring cities, but there was no large-scale warfare. Over time, a variety of kings in the various cities claimed hegemony, and these reigns are recorded in the mythical and factual king's list.[31]

By the time Enheduanna became high priestess at Ur, the Sumerian pantheon was firmly in place with power centered in the male gods: An, the calm, authoritative god of heaven and the numinous power in the sky; Enlil, god of the air between heaven and earth, especially the moist spring winds, whose authority is expressed with energy and force by a storm;[32] and Enki, god of wisdom, magic, and of the sweet waters. In contrast, Enheduanna chose to elevate a goddess to the supreme position in the pantheon, one who combines a paradoxical blend of power and mercy. Inanna's forces are the cycles of nature that can be devastating or beneficent. All life, whether material, psychological, or spiritual, is ruled by the principle of ebb and flow, and Inanna is mistress of change.

Enheduanna's surfacing in our century after four thousand years of silence corresponds with an increased global awareness and concern for women's rights. Even though Enheduanna's writings are filtered through an evolving male-dominated society, her poetry seems to describe what must have been the core beliefs of the ancient Neolithic goddess-dominated religions. Many elements of her Inanna fit the assumptions of a nature-based religion depicted in the ancient artifacts.

4

⌄

Unearthing
Enheduanna

In 1922 archaeologists from the University of Pennsylvania and the British Museum began a joint venture to uncover the ancient city of Ur buried under a mound of sand in southern Iraq. Their discoveries would change the world's knowledge and perception of history and prehistory. The rich finds from their excavations illuminate thirty-five hundred years of early civilization, starting with the first villages built on the edge of salt marshes around 4000 B.C.E., in what is now modern Iraq, and continuing through layers of occupation whose existence had only been imagined. Ur was a center of the Sumerian civilization that flourished along the Euphrates not far from its confluence with the Tigris where the two rivers formed a huge delta at the northern-most end of the Persian Gulf.

The expedition, led by the young Englishman Leonard Woolley, excavated the mound at Ur for twelve seasons. Often the conditions in which his team worked were horrendous. Ur is located on the edge of the desert between Baghdad and the Persian Gulf, ten miles west of the Euphrates. The workers were plagued by blinding dust storms and torrential rains. Woolley and his wife, Katherine, who worked with the expedition and was responsible for drawing many of the artifacts, lived in a house made of bricks dug out of the excavated buildings. Before returning one season, a co-worker, Max Mallowan, prepared the house for the Woolleys' arrival. He wrote that "owing to the unusually heavy sandstorms of last summer (the house) was completely buried and had to be excavated, 100 men at this for four days." [1] Mallowan gives a vivid picture of life in the camp:

We were subject to violent sandstorms as well as to heavy rain. We often had to brush the sand away from our field cards as we struggled to finish off a job before dismissing the men, and there were some days when food, drink, and everything else, including bathwater and beds were sand laden. The local bread too was a mixture of sand and dough, nor had conditions changed in four thousand years, for we often found that the teeth of the ancient inhabitants had been ground down through masticating grit. When it rained hard we were isolated, and the desert could then appear as a vast lake. I remember one November when we were hit by a veritable monsoon, and outside the house we had to work waist deep in water with as many men as we could muster building up a protective bund to save our property against the flood.[2]

In their third season of work, the excavators found a small, round alabaster disc near the temple residence of the high priestess of the moon god Nanna. The disc, depicting a priestess presiding over a libation ritual, was broken and had been deliberately defaced. When the pieces were mended, an inscription appeared on the back:

> Enheduanna, true lady of Nanna, wife of Nanna,
> daughter of Sargon, King of all, in the temple of
> Inanna [of Ur, a dais you built (and) "Dais,"
> table of heaven (An)] you called it.[3]

The excavators had discovered the portrait of Enheduanna, high priestess of the moon god and the first poet of record. Her writings are the earliest work of an author known to be a historical figure and identified by name in the poems and hymns she wrote.

On the disc Enheduanna named her father Sargon, "King of All." Before the disc's discovery, the excavators did not know whether the legendary Sargon was historical or mythical. No one had ever heard of Enheduanna. In the seventy-five years since the excavation, scholars have dug and deciphered thousands of baked clay tablets and artifacts that have greatly expanded our knowledge of Mesopotamia, the "cradle of civilization." Among the five thousand or more Mesopotamian literary tablets, three long poems to Inanna, three poems to Nanna, and forty-two temple hymns are Enheduanna's work.[4]

To uncover the layers of the city, dedicated and persistent workers had to dig and sift through tons of sand under the most difficult conditions. Working under the constant press of nature's harsh forces in southern

13.(a) Limestone disk of Enheduanna, from Ur, diameter 26 cm. Courtesy of the University
of Pennsylvania Museum, Philadelphia, (neg. #139330).

Iraq, the team discovered treasure after treasure. After finding the temple
of the moon god Nanna and the buildings in the surrounding compound,
someone discovered the shattered pieces of the alabaster disc in the pub-
lic area of the high priestess's residence, the **gipar**. There it had rested
for thousands of years while storms, rain, and dust battered the mound
at Ur, century after century. Woolley describes the find:

in the Moon-goddess' temple we found a sadly-battered alabaster disc on one
side of which was carved in relief just such a scene of worship by the High Priest-

(b) The unrestored disc of Enheduanna. Courtesy of the University of Pennsylvania Museum, Philadelphia, (neg. #139229).

ess as was given on the Lagash plaque, but an inscription on the back tells us that the principal figure with her flounced dress and high conical hat is none other than En-he-du-an-na, daughter of King Sargon of Akkad. It was an astonishing piece of luck to get this personal evidence regarding Sargon . . . ; now we have En-he-du-an-na, and she is a very real person; she lived at Ur and she had her court there, as beseemed a princess.[5]

Enheduanna is the central figure on the round, 25.6 cm diameter disc. In Sumerian art, the round form of the disc is unique and may take its shape from the full moon of Nanna.[6] Enheduanna and Inanna both are connected to the moon god. Enheduanna is the high priestess of Nanna, the principal god of the moon, and Inanna is the daughter of the Sumerian moon couple, Nanna and Ningal. Sumerian scholar Joan Goodnick Westenholz describes the disc:

On the obverse, it reveals Enheduanna, accompanied by two persons in front of whom is a naked male functionary performing a libation on an altar (or more probably a plant stand) before the incorrectly restored ziggurat. She is clothed in a fleeced wool garment; her hair is worn loose with locks of curls flowing down her back and over her shoulder. Upon her head has been restored the distinctive rolled-brim cap but a high conical hat (polos?) seems to be depicted on the pre-restoration disc. She is shown in profile with her right arm raised in a gesture of salutation.[7]

Enheduanna's right hand is raised before her face in a gesture known from other texts and carvings. In the poem "Lady of Largest Heart," Enheduanna describes Inanna performing a ritual, "hands then folded at her nose." The Sumerian verb "to greet," **kiri$_4$ šu-gal$_2$**, literally means "to let the hand be at the nose." Irene Winter says of this gesture on the disc, "her right hand bent at the elbow, hand raised before the face, in a well-known gesture of pious greeting, comparable to those depicted in presentation scenes, from Ur III seals to the Code of Hammurabi."[8] Behind Enheduanna are two attendants, both striking similar poses with their right hands. One is carrying a vessel, possibly an incense burner used in this dedication ritual. Winter says the apparently bald attendants are probably male, although on the prerestoration disc the only surviving head of an attendant is quite broken.

The figure of Enheduanna on the disc is noticeably larger than the others; her head actually touches the upper margin of the frieze. Winter notes that "this correlation between rank and relative size . . . first appears in Mesopotamia in the Early Dynastic III period."[9] She wears a rolled-brimmed hat, the **aga** "crown," special headgear of the high priestess. In the poem "The Exaltation," Enheduanna says of her usurper, "he robbed me/ of the true crown (**aga**)/ of the High Priestess."

The disc commemorates an event in which Enheduanna dedicated a dais in the temple of Inanna in the city of Ur. The procession pictured on the disc must depict the ritual inauguration of the new dais, or raised platform which Enheduanna calls "table of heaven." Winter says, "the dais is frequently mentioned as allocating sacred space, on which kings or gods are seated." [10]

On the disc in what Westenholz says is "the one extant original inscription from her hands," [11] Enheduanna describes herself as "true lady of Nanna, wife of Nanna." Enheduanna had been appointed to her position as high priestess to Nanna by her father the king. Her appointment followed a tradition that may have begun hundreds of years earlier in which the daughter of the king became the high priestess of the moon god in Ur. We will explore this history in more detail later.

Enheduanna's appointment was unique in several ways. By the time of her installation, Sargon had united all the warring city-states of Mesopotamia under one central government in the northern city of Akkad, and this was the first successful unification of the southern cities under a single administrative organization.[12] The traditionally nomadic, Semitic-speaking tribes that had entered Sumer from the west, from whom Sargon traced his lineage, crossed the deserts of present-day Syria and the Arabian peninsula, and lived peacefully with the Sumerians at least from the fourth millennium, possibly earlier. There is no evidence of ethnic or racial conflict. Joan Oates describes the varied mix that made up the Sumerians.

the term 'Sumerian' . . . is generally used to describe the common culture of a population composed of mixed linguistic elements, and there is some reason to suppose that its ethnic composition was equally diverse. From the time of the earliest records, there appears to be no social distinction in Sumer between persons bearing Semitic and Sumerian names . . . Since we cannot recognize any intrusive element among this medley, it seems probable that we must attribute it to a mingling of stocks in prehistoric times.[13]

The language of the Semitic speakers came to be known as Akkadian, after Sargon's capitol city of Akkad. The Akkadians eventually adopted the Sumerians' cuneiform script to write their own language. In the Early Dynastic period (2960–2360 B.C.E.), a number of Semitic speaking kings had gained power. Sargon maintained a singular determination to transfer the center of power to the north, away from the southern cities. Revolts sprang up sporadically as the cities of the south tried to free themselves from Akkadian domination during Sargon's long reign as well as those of his sons and nephew who succeeded him.

Some scholars believe Sargon appointed his daughter high priestess in Ur, in order to enlist the support of the established religious hierarchy.[14] Ur, where she would live, was a city in the south, the heartland of the Sumerian culture, while Akkad, his base, lay far away in the north, in the vicinity of present-day Baghdad. With the installation of his daughter in an important religious office, Sargon hoped to exercise more control over the southern provinces with their predominantly Sumerian population.

"True lady of Nanna, wife of Nanna" Enheduanna calls herself on the disc. Nanna's wife in Sumerian myth was the moon goddess Ningal. As high priestess, Enheduanna bridged the mysterious space between mortals and the gods. In the yearly sacred marriage ritual she "became" Ningal and prepared to meet Nanna on the consecrated bed in the temple. Because of her role as Nanna's wife, she was called "**nin-dinger**," "lady who is a god."

Thus, Enheduanna describes her identity in three ways on the disc. In her role as priestess she is "wife of Nanna." Next, she is the mortal "daughter of Sargon, King of All." And finally, she reveals her devotion to Inanna as she dedicates the dais to the goddess.

Each of the three poems in this book, "Inanna and Ebih," "Lady of Largest Heart," and "The Exaltation of Inanna," is a song of praise to Inanna. Though her public, priestly duties focused on the moon couple, Nanna and Ningal, Enheduanna's private devotion was to Inanna.

The piecing together of the disc's fragments gave us not only historical evidence of this priestess but an actual picture of her, carved in alabaster, performing a ritual to her beloved Inanna. This rare find, along with the later discovery of her poetry, is the legacy of an ancient flesh and blood woman who struggled, as her poetry shows, to make sense of her life and her suffering. She left us a record of one woman's ability to understand and to transform the vicissitudes of her fate through worship of that complex, enigmatic goddess, Inanna. Enheduanna provided a glimpse into a hidden world where ancient women encountered the sustaining matrix of their devotion in a form they associated intimately with their bodies, the goddesses.

CHAPTER

5

⌄ ⌄

Enheduanna's
Life Story

Enheduanna's story begins before she was born. She became a princess, and eventually high priestess, by virtue of her father's rise to power as he conquered and claimed kingship over all Mesopotamia. To place Enheduanna in history, we must first understand her relationship to her father.

In the Akkadian version of the Sargon legend, Sargon was born in a town on the Euphrates, Azupiranu, "Saffron Town," an ancient center for the harvesting of the tiny orange stigma of the *Crocus sativus* that yields the pungent spice, saffron, and forms the base for the rich yellow and burnt orange dye. Sargon's father has been identified variously over the centuries, as a man named La'ibum, or as a gardener, or as a person unknown even to Sargon.[1] According to legend, Sargon's mother was a priestess who bore her child in secret.[2] She placed her baby in a reed basket lined with pitch and pushed the little boat out onto the river.[3] A gardener, drawing water from the river to irrigate his date palm trees, pulled the basket ashore. This man, Aqqi, raised the boy as his own and taught him the gardening profession.[4] As a young man, Sargon claimed to have won the favor of the goddess Ishtar, the Semitic name for Inanna. Perhaps because of this divine intercession or through the influence of a priestess to Ishtar, he became a servant in the household of the Sumerian king, Ur-Zababa of Kish. Kish was the capital of Sumer about sixty miles south of the present city of Baghdad. Kish was a prominent city in the five hundred-year Early Dynastic period that saw a succession of kings rule over Sumer. Inanna, in her large temple, was tutelary deity of

43

Kish. She gave her chosen kings the title, "King of Kish," and they, in turn, called themselves "spouse of Inanna."

Sargon soon attained the position of cupbearer to the king, putting him in charge of drink offerings to the gods. Later, refusing Ur-Zababa's order to "change the drink offering of E-sagila,"[5] a libation to the god, Sargon broke with the king. According to tradition, Enlil, the great god of the spring wind and storm, and the god whose approval was necessary to legitimate the earthly king, was disturbed by a cultic offense, perhaps Ur-Zababa's insistence on changing the traditional drink offering. Enlil then bestowed his divine blessing on Sargon, leaving the old king without legitimacy.

In the Sumerian version of the Sargon legend, the gods An and Enlil decree the end of the reign of Ur-Zababa and make way for Sargon, cupbearer to the king, to replace him.[6] The Sumerian tale is vivid and dramatic. With "Holy Inanna unceasingly working behind the scenes,"[7] Sargon plots Ur-Zababa's death. The king "knows it in his heart" and is terrified.[8]

'Like a lion' sprinkling the inside of his legs with urine in which there was plenty of fresh blood he moaned and gasped like a struggling salt-water fish.[9]

The frightened king lays a trap for Sargon, but to no avail. "(D)estiny determined by the gods is unavoidable and not to be resisted."[10]

After leaving the king's service, Sargon began to develop a following of his own. In a location archaeologists have yet to discover, he established a city on the Euphrates, not far from Kish, which he named Agade (or Akkad).

Legend interweaves with history. At some point Sargon conferred on himself the name "Sharruken," later changed to Sargon, which means "the king is legitimate, the legitimate king."[11] This name declared to all that he, and no one else, occupied the center of power.

From the stronghold of Akkad, Sargon led his armies to conquer all the city-states of Mesopotamia, and he was the first to unite the southern cities under one central rule.[12] He defeated Lugalzaggesi of Umma, who had made his own attempt to unite the southern cities. Lugalzaggesi, a particularly destructive ruler, had "burned, looted and destroyed practically all the holy places of Lagash,"[13] behavior the Sumerians associated only with barbarians. The Sumerians may have welcomed their new king, if only temporarily.

14. Cast copper head of Sargon or Naram-Sin found in the Ishtar Temple at Nineveh. Height 36.6 cm. Courtesy of the Iraq Museum, Baghdad.

After securing the Mesopotamian cities, Sargon ventured beyond the traditional borders into present-day Syria traveling all the way to the Taurus Mountains in Turkey. He controlled northern Mesopotamia, including the mountain borders to the north and east. His ships docked in the Persian Gulf at its many ports. He may have established outposts in Egypt, Ethiopia, and India. The Sumerian cities were garrisoned with Akkadian troops. He boasted that fifty-four hundred men ate daily before him.[14] At one point his kingdom included most of the known world.

Enheduanna was born into the household of this ambitious, charismatic man, the only daughter among Sargon's five children. Although Sargon was married to a Semitic-speaking Akkadian, Tashlutum, she may not have been Enheduanna's mother. Sargon probably had other wives, and he certainly kept concubines. Some scholars believe Enheduanna's mother was Sumerian, judging from the poet's elegant use of that language.[15]

Enheduanna grew to maturity in the palace at the time of Sargon's expanding political power. Her father's return from victory in a foreign land was a commonplace scene for her as a young girl. She witnessed the Akkadian people's adulation of her father and the triumphant celebrations in the palace. She knew that her uncles and cousins governed the cities her father had conquered. She heard about Uruk, Ur, and Umma, cities to the south, whose king, Lugalzaggesi, fought against her father's army. She knew these people were Sumerians and she was Akkadian.

Enheduanna grew up in the midst of a creative evolution of some of the most basic cultural constructs of her society. For the five hundred years before Sargon came to power, Sumerians had dominated the region. Sumerian was the principal language spoken, and Sumerians had invented and developed the pictographic script that was the basis for cuneiform. This script represented the first-known successful attempt at writing a language used in all areas of common life, economic, political, literary, and religious.[16] A powerful, creative energy drove Sumerian culture. In these five hundred years before Sargon, the Sumerian influence spread throughout Mesopotamia and into bordering lands. People in this area worshiped the Sumerian gods and built the traditional ziggurat temples. The Sumerians developed a body of myth, song, and story, mostly tales of the gods. Such powerful cities as Ur, Uruk, Lagash, Kish, and Nippur in the south engaged in extensive trade with cities in the midsection of the country and in the north and with settlements in present-day Turkey, Iran, the Persian Gulf region, east to the Indus basin and west to the Mediterranean.

When Sargon came to power, he ushered in a series of cultural changes that altered the traditional Sumerian way of life and brought this Sumerian-dominated period, the Early Dynastic, to an end. Akkadian replaced Sumerian as the primary spoken language, and for the first time, a Semitic language, Old Akkadian, was written using the cuneiform script invented by the Sumerians. The traditional Sumerian city-states in the south lost power and influence as Sargon moved the center of power to the midsection of the country, to Akkad.

Now the creative energy was in the hands of the Semites. The written tablets of this period used the new script in a form J. N. Postgate describes "of great regularity and formality."[17] C. J. Gadd recounts that the scribes, using a fine clay, wrote the cuneiform signs "with a care and beauty which were not matched again until the Assyrian calligraphers were set to work upon the library tablets of Ashurbanipal." [18] Another striking change took place, according to Postgate, in the system of weights and measures that in the past had differed from city to city. Now "measures of length, area, dry and liquid capacity, and probably also weight were integrated into a single logical system which remained the standard for a thousand years and more." [19] These changes were made possible by the new centralized government.

The world depicted in Akkadian art had a new cast. In the carved reliefs of this era, individual soldiers fashioned with a freedom of movement, are slim, well balanced, and realistically portrayed. Crowds of the enemy are no longer aligned in identical repetition; rather, individuals are posed in various attitudes of fear, anguish, or subjugation. The Semitic artists, energized by their king's elevation of the Akkadians to the pinnacle of power, were inspired to create new cultural expressions that depicted the individual.

In the midst of these exciting changes the princess Enheduanna grew into womanhood. Enheduanna's life began in privilege and wealth. As daughter of the king, she had a part to play in implementing the enormous changes her father had initiated. In time, Enheduanna's father appointed her high priestess of the moon god Nanna at the temple in Ur, far to the south of her home in Akkad. During her long life, a close family member ruled as king. According to Maisels, Sargon set an example his successors would follow: maintaining power and thriving "by monopolizing exchange and extracting tribute." [20] Enheduanna's brother Rimush, who succeeded Sargon, left inscriptions declaring victory over an uprising of southern cities as well as over the eastern province of Elam and Tell Brak in present-day Syria. Rimush may have been murdered by his older brother and successor Manishtushu, who struggled with many of the same problems of rebellion in the homeland and preservation of hegemony over the foreign territories. Manishtushu was also murdered.

Manishtushu's son Naram-Sin was the true progeny of his grandfather Sargon, culminating his extraordinary reign of power by declaring himself a god. Gadd notes that documents from Agade do not provide evidence of the dominance of the former Sumerian temple economy.[21] Along with Naram-Sin's deification, this political shift pits the traditional role of the temple against the secular rule of the king. By calling himself "god of Akkad," Naram-Sin claimed for himself the city god's land and possessions, traditionally the property of the temple. Complicating this picture is the fact that the city "god" of Akkad was the goddess Ishtar, the Akkadian Inanna. This struggle between the religious sphere, its temples and personnel, and that of the secular rulers, now boasting some fifty years of dynastic power, is further evidence of the change in cultural institutions and the consciousness of the period.[22] It may be that Enheduanna's elevation of Inanna in her poems to a central position among the gods was a dissident act protesting the intrusion of the king into the domain of the religion.

Finally Enheduanna took the new consciousness of the individual, which we see in Akkadian art, and wrote about herself. "I, I am Enheduanna," she says. Her poetry was inspired by the most intimate nuances of feeling. She explored the transformative role emotion plays in the individual. Now at the dawn of the twenty-first century, we are only beginning to understand the full weight emotion and image carry in the human psyche. Enheduanna opened herself to these insights over four thousand years ago.

6

◣◢

The High Priestess
at Ur

Exactly when Sargon appointed his daughter to the office of high priest-
ess to the moon god Nanna at Ur is uncertain. Sargon ruled for fifty-
five years; his two sons ruled one after the other for another twenty-
two years. Sargon's powerful grandson, Naram-Sin, followed and ruled
for thirty-six years. As Enheduanna was high priestess when Naram-
Sin was in power, Sargon must have appointed her to the office late in
his reign "a judgement borne out by the glyptic evidence," says William
Hallo.[1] Her position as high priestess in the south gave her influence in
the most central organizing institution of the Sumerian people's culture,
their religion.

Every indication suggests that Sargon appointed his daughter to the
post to help solidify his control over the restless and rebellious popula-
tions of southern Sumerian cities, whose traditions differed from those
of the Akkadians in the north. Enheduanna stepped into a cultic office
familiar to the Sumerians, one they revered and honored.[2] Her appoint-
ment by Sargon followed a tradition that had been in place, in some form,
for hundreds of years. Irene Winter argues that "the ritual office of en-
priestess of Nanna had to have predated Enheduanna, occurring at least
as early as the Early Dynastic III period," and goes on to say "since the
really formative period for urban Mesopotamian cult activity seems to
have been the Uruk/Jemdet Nasr period, it would not be entirely un-
toward to assume that the office (of the en-priestess and priest) would
have been in existence as long as the religious system."[3]

In the Sumerian religious practice, male en-priests served the goddesses, while female en-priestesses served the gods. There were en-priests and priestesses in a number of Mesopotamian cities, for example in the Uruk temples of Inanna and of An. These priests and priestesses served the great gods almost exclusively, not the minor goddesses and gods.[4] Evidence of the cultic tradition in the moon-god temple is consistent over the ages so that, as Mark Hall says, "evidence from earlier periods indicates the existence of traditions more fully documented in later periods."[5]

As already stated, the cult of the moon god appears to reach back into great antiquity. Hall places Nanna/Suen in the preliterate, nomadic period based on his position as god of the herds.[6]

The oldest attested appearance of the name Nanna is as a personal name on Jemdet Nasr period tablets from Uruk.[7] Nanna is the name of the moon god preferred in Sumerian personal names, while the Akkadian-speaking Semitic people preferred the name Suen. Suen occurs in Ugaritic and South Arabian texts as well as in cuneiform Akkadian in the "earliest written sources and points to a place of origin outside of Mesopotamia."[8] A third name for the moon god is Ashimbabbar. It is unclear whether this name referred to a moon god distinct from Nanna/Suen. This name appears on lists of gods from the pre-Sargonic period. While the meaning of the words "Nanna" and "Suen" are not known, Ashimbabbar could mean "who walks alone" or "bull who walks alone" in Sumerian, as well as "rising brilliantly" in Akkadian.[9]

The earliest texts list certain professional titles related to personnel connected to the moon god. Among them is a phrase very similar to the one found on the disc of Enheduanna, "**munus-nunuz-zi-**[d]**nanna**," "true lady of Nanna" or as Westenholz has interpreted the phrase, "Hen of Nanna," a title Ningal "bestows . . . on Enheduanna" that signifies her role as sexual partner to Nanna.[10] The phrase in the earlier text, "**munus-zi-**[d]**nanna**," likely refers to a priestess who served in Nanna's temple in a role similar to that of the high priestess.[11]

However the role had been envisioned in the past, Enheduanna defined it in a new way with her powerful intellect, her creative gifts, and her capacity for leadership. Unlike her predecessors she could use the effective tool of the written word to spread her influence and her beliefs. The forty-two hymns she wrote to temples throughout the country must have been read to worshipers periodically, establishing Enheduanna as a voice of authority, someone to whom they looked for leadership (see Chapter 7). Enheduanna's three poems to Inanna effectively defined a new hierarchy of the gods even though her theology was couched in traditional beliefs about Inanna. Enheduanna used her office to create and promote her own point of view, preserving her texts for the first time in history on durable clay tablets. The precedent she established strongly influenced the priestesses who followed her. Kings, who had the power to confer descriptive names to each year of their reigns, frequently chose a high priestess' name, after her inauguration, to designate the year, implying that her installation was the year's most important event.[12] William Hallo says that the prestige and influence of the high priestesses during the Sargonic dynasty "was in some sense unequaled in the Ancient Near East." [13] Hall confirms this, saying, "The most significant activity undertaken by the kings of Akkad and their successors for the cult of the moon god was the installation of the en-priestess at Ur." [14] Enheduanna originated and established this new role. Perhaps because of her great prestige and the significant political power of Ur after the fall of the Akkad dynasty, the cult of the moon god at Ur became even more central in the subsequent Ur III period.[15]

The Moon Temple at Ur

While Enheduanna's influence was felt throughout the country, the locus of her activity was in Ur. As was traditional in Mesopotamian city-states, the temple was the center not only of religious life but of economic and social life as well. The temple became an institution that Maisels describes as essential: "the temple organization which, uniting in itself cosmological and productive functions, facilitated the adaption of post-Neolithic settlers to the demanding ecology of the alluvium and its contiguous semi-arid extensions." [16] Evolving from the great houses, "the supra-household basis of social storage crystallized into the temples at the nodes of agricultural and social reproduction. In turn the temples . . . served as the cores of the synoecism that crystalized into cities." [17] The T-form building of Neolithic Samarra evolved into the typical Sumerian household, the **é-gal,** which evolved into the temple, also called **é-gal.**

Conflicts between the priestly administrators of the extensive economic holdings of the temple and private landowners arose early in city formation. Falkenstein suspects that the earliest temples owned all of the surrounding land. Urukagina, the last Early Dynastic king before Sargon, tried to return privately held lands back to Ningirsu, the chief god of Lagash.[18] This conflict was intense during the Sargon dynasty and culminated with Naram-Sin's declaration that he was "god of Akkad," whereby he assumed control of the temple as well as the secular political sector.

As the en-priestess, Enheduanna managed the extensive agricultural enterprise on the land around the temple. The term "**en**" refers to the priestly management of the fecundity of the land. The cultivation of crops, the care of livestock, and even a fishing industry occupied large numbers of people working for the temple. Their occupations included "plowmen, ox-drivers; herders of cattle, sheep, goats, asses, she-asses, and pigs; . . . gardeners . . . ; fishermen, who are subdivided into 'freshwater fishermen,' 'brackish-water fishermen,' and 'sea fishermen.' "[19] Others were engaged as "bakers and cooks, butchers, brewers, and leather-workers . . . woodworkers, builders, smiths, silversmiths, and stoneworkers."[20] Falkenstein, speaking of the temple at Lagash (not that far removed or different from the one at Ur), says all this activity meant that every family was in some way employed by the temple.[21]

These estates provided the high priestesses considerable economic independence, enabling them to make loans from the temple treasury.[22] The temple staff and employees included a large portion of the city's population, for all of whom the high priestess was responsible.[23] Her title, en-priestess, designates a singular purpose: she is the lady who engenders abundance, the ruler over prosperity. Evidence from a later time indicates that the high priestess was active at many levels of economic and social life and could own property and transact business in cities other than the primary cult residence.[24] To manage these duties the high priestess had a large personal staff. Cylinder seals of three of Enheduanna's servants were found in the cemetery of Ur. The seals belonged to Ada, her steward; Dingir-palil, possibly her hairdresser; and the scribe Kitushdug.[25]

Enheduanna also directed activity organized around the liturgical year, guiding a large staff of temple personnel—priests, priestesses, weavers, scribes, cooks, gardeners, and merchants—through the necessary preparations and duties required for the enactment of prescribed rituals. All this activity took place for the sake of one principal outcome: the assurance of gifts of bounty and goodness from the moon god and goddess, Nanna and Ningal. As high priestess, Enheduanna held the office that directed rituals pleasing to the gods and therefore kept the people safe within a contained, dependable, orderly, prosperous universe.

The Moon Couple Nanna and Ningal

The Sumerian high priestess and the temple personnel at Ur expended tremendous energy and resources on the care and well-being of the moon couple, Nanna and Ningal. While the first mention of Nanna is from the Early Dynastic period, the god Sumerians called Nanna merely stepped into a role and adopted a complexity of meanings that had probably developed in remote antiquity.

Paleolithic markings on animal bones and horns inform us that our ancestors watched the moon carefully. The moon's phases are precisely recorded on finds from this era, an activity Alexander Marschack, who deciphered the markings, says was part of a general myth of these people.[26] Given this meticulous observation, we can be sure early people noted that women's monthly bleeding occurred in synchrony with the 29.5 day cycle of the moon. This equation must have posed a profound mystery to the developing minds of our ancestors. With little to guide them in culture or history, they must have seen the correspondence between women and the moon as a sacred sign of connection to the unknown surrounding them. The moon became a goddess or a god to be worshiped, and women became mediators of great spiritual power.

Likewise, throughout Sumer, the moon was observed nightly, both for setting ritual observances and for calculating time. The "day of the new moon," u_4-**sakar**, was particularly significant. On this day each month a festival was celebrated called èš-èš. This festival's observance also took place on the following days of the major phases of the moon, the seventh, and fifteenth days. Offerings to the moon god included bulls, sheep, lambs and kids, as well as baskets of dates, pomegranates, and other fruits. These highly organized festivals involved carefully kept records of all offerings. So important were these celebrations at Ur that the costs were borne by the Ur temple as well as by the king and the chief leaders (**ensi**) of other cities who took turns providing some of the necessary supplies.[27]

The phases of the moon after the full moon were not celebrated. The waning moon seemed to represent the moon god's journey toward the underworld, where on the day of the moon's disappearance, u_4-ná-a, "day of the lying down of the moon," Nanna visited Lord Nergal, god of the underworld and "decreed fates for the dead."[28]

In Iraq the new moon's position in the sky is horizontal. In Sumer this appearance of the moon resembled the crown or horns of Nanna. Correspondingly, the shape of the ubiquitous boats, called in Sumerian **mà-gur**, the primary mode of transportation through the marshes of the delta, still copy the crescent shape of the new moon. Nanna was thought to ride the crescent moon-boat of heaven on its monthly course.[29]

Woolley's discovery of the compound of the moon god's temple in Ur has been studied by scholars ever since. While a clear understanding of the use of the many buildings remains elusive, a general consensus has emerged. The compound contained a raised terrace on which the ziggurat stood. The whole terrace, surrounded by a wall, "was divided into two separate religious precincts," described by Hall:

the one covering the whole northwest side of the terrace was the domain of Nanna; the other on the southeast side belonged to his consort, Ningal. The dividing line between the two and possibly their common meeting ground was the ziggurat in the center . . . the temple which once stood at the top of the ziggurat was their common domain where the two were worshipped together.[30]

Nanna's appearance in 2600 B.C.E. was one of many such appearances by a moon god in human history. He manifested an accretion of ancient meanings that connected humankind to moon worship. Nanna's epithets were both celestial and earthbound. As the moon he rose at night, illuminating the darkness, "the proud one coming forth from the azure sky," wearing the crescent moon as a crown. On earth he was the divine shepherd as well as a "frisky calf"; in his beneficence he lavished cream and cheese, milk and butter on his devoted.[31] Wolfgang Heimpel suggests that Nanna's many cows in their celestial form appeared as stars in the sky with the moon as shepherd, leading to the designation of our galaxy as the Milky Way.[32]

While Inanna is the goddess of the planet Venus, she is also the eldest child of the moon couple. According to Enheduanna's description, Inanna is the ebb and flow at the heart of the cosmic plan, and thus she is another symbol, like the moon, of the natural order of change. As the

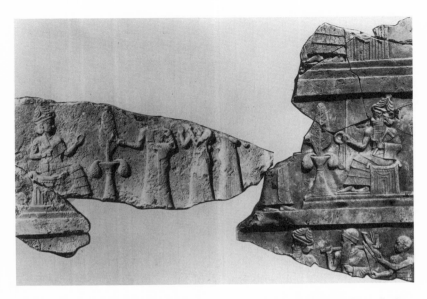

15. UR Nammu Stele Fragment. Nanna and Ningal receive offerings from the king and give the order to build the ziggurat of Ur. Courtesy of the University of Pennsylvania Museum, Philadelphia, (neg. #140070).

epitome of ebb and flow, she holds in her wide arms all the opposites the world's natural cycles exhibit: scarcity and plenty, dark and light, violence and tenderness, death and life.

Unlike Inanna, Enheduanna is not a daughter of the moon. Rather she is the moon's bride, playing the part of Ningal in the sacred marriage ritual (see below). As one high priestess after Enheduanna wrote, she is "a (woman with) loins suitable by (their) purity for the *entu*-ship."[33] In the sacred marriage ritual Enheduanna became Ningal, the female moon. She enacted the joining together of god and goddess, male and female, heaven and earth that showered the blessings of fertility and prosperity for the New Year.

One of Enheduanna's primary functions as high priestess was to care for Ningal, to keep her content, well fed, and beneficent to her adoring public. Ningal, probably represented by a statue of the goddess, received the most devoted attention. Much of the time and energy of certain temple personnel was spent caring for the goddess who lived in her

own quarters within the sacred building, home of the high priestess, the
gipar. Weadock describes Ningal's temple quarters:

> Its central court surrounded by rooms is similar in plan to those in private houses,
> but to it have been added features found only in the house of a deity: the ritual
> washing place where the priest or worshipper might purify himself before ap-
> proaching the divine owner of the house; the bases upon which stood stelae com-
> memorating the pious acts of such important attendants as the king and the *entu;*
> and the benches against the wall serving as seats for the divine administrators
> of the temple affairs. Such features as the storage jars, the weaver's pit, and the
> economic tablets attest to the varied activities involved in running an estate, and
> the cella and the ante-cella correspond to the rooms set aside in a private house
> for the owner of the house. Here the goddess sat on a raised dais and her visitors
> paid court to her effigy.[34]

The goddess Ningal played an essential role in the cult of the moon
god at Ur, the only city with which she is associated. In later texts she
was called "mother of Ur," while a hymn to Ningal is listed as early as
the archaic texts from the Fara period, around 2500 B.C.E.[35]

Ningal was fed daily meals, a "regular offering" of "beer, flour, bread
and meat."[36] She was adorned with jewels and clothing woven and manu-
factured in the temple workshops. She received gifts of "combs, coffers,
and various vessels of silver and gold."[37] In the archives of the **gá-nun-
mah,** the storehouse of the Ningal temple, offerings were carefully re-
corded including butter, cheese, milk, dates and oil, white beans, lentils,
coriander, cassia, pine nuts, honey, grain, and "a small amount of ordi-
nary oil for the leather door hinges."[38] All the people held Ningal in rev-
erence, because their fate depended upon her. Only she could receive the
great Nanna in the sacred marriage ritual.

Ningal's menstrual cycle was charted, as was Inanna's (see below).
In an interesting bit of detective work, Claus Wilcke found the verb
root for 'a menstruating woman' in the name of Ishara, the goddess
Ishtar/Inanna in her mother aspect. Never a mother, Ishtar becomes
Ishara when she gives birth in the great Akkadian creation epic, Athraha-
sis. Wilcke found the verb root *rš*, "to menstruate," "to be in childbed,"
switched in Ishara's name to *šr*. The related Akkadian verb *haraštu* means
"to bind" and is used to refer to the cloth-binding used by menstruating
women.[39] These goddesses, as prototypes of women, carried the moon's
29.5 day cycle in their bodies.

The numinosity of the correlation between the moon's cycle and women's cycles has been observed in rituals of many cultures. In her book *Blood, Bread, and Roses,* Judy Grahn attributes the origin of ritual, and even the beginning of culture, to our ancestors' discovery of the correspondence of the menstrual cycle with the phases of the moon. Grahn compared the rituals of menstrual seclusion recorded in the last two centuries by James Frazer, Jane C. Goodale, Margaret Mead, and others. The menstruating woman, particularly at menarche, was commonly required to observe three taboos: she must not see light, not touch water, and not touch the earth. The profound power of menstrual blood that necessitated these taboos was related to its appearance in synchrony with the phases of the moon. The woman was therefore obligated to observe practices that would contain and harness the immensity of this power, for the gods can as easily destroy as create. These early observances grew into the first rituals. Grahn draws on accounts of menstrual ritual from all over the world as she describes the carefully devised practices through which women contained this mystery.[40]

The great ritual for which Ningal was so carefully tended was the sacred marriage. This festival to assure the continued fertility of the land probably took place at the time of the New Year, after the harvest. The culmination of the ritual was the joining of the goddess, represented by the high priestess, and the god, represented by the king, in sacred sexual intercourse, an act of such potency that the Sumerians believed it sparked the regeneration of all agricultural life.

The Sacred Marriage Ritual

The sacred marriage is often referred to in songs and poems but its actual occurrence is difficult to verify in offering texts or ritual descriptions. The most explicit evidence of a ritual of sacred marriage appears in two Sumerian hymns from the Ur III period: one hymn comes from the reign of King Shulgi of Ur (2050 B.C.E.) and another from the period of King Iddendagan of Isin's reign (1950 B.C.E.). Some scholars question whether such evidence from the Sargonic period was actual or symbolic.[41] Weadock firmly asserts that it was actual and that "the celebration of the sacred marriage between Ningal and Sin (Nanna) was . . . the supreme purpose of the Ningal temple."[42] In descriptions of the moon god under various names and locals, only Nanna at Ur is related to Ningal in an erotic manner. Weadock describes Woolley's discovery, in an important room of the Ningal temple, of a "low platform" Woolley thought might serve as the base for a bed. A stele of a later en-priestess, Enanedu, mentions a bed of Ningal encrusted with gold.[43] The Ningal temple itself was referred to as the **é-nun**, a word Weadock traces to a part of the house in which people might spend the night.[44] Because the ritual involved the high priestess in such an intimate way, it is worthwhile to look at it more closely.

Carvings of copulating couples, some of which scholars see as representing ritual intercourse, have been found even in Neolithic sites in ancient Mesopotamia (9000 to 5000 B.C.E.),[45] suggesting that the Sumerian sacred marriage ritual is in some way related to this long tradition. The first historical evidence of the sacred marriage ritual comes from the Early Dynastic period, from a text that refers to the union of King Enmerkar with Inanna.[46] This text substantiates the theory that goddesses other than Ningal took part in a sacred marriage ritual in their own temples. In the later Ur III period, the ritual was the subject of a number of royal hymns. Jacob Klein says of the sacred marriage:

This ritual probably originated in ancient Uruk, where the deified king Dumuzi (biblical Tammuz) married Inanna and thus entered the Sumerian pantheon as the vegetation and fertility god. The sacred marriage in Ur's Third Dynasty period was celebrated during the New Year festival when the king, representing Dumuzi, united with a priestess, representing Inanna. Their union was believed to revive the forces of life and fertility in nature and society, and to ensure abundance for Sumer in the subsequent year.[47]

Jerrold Cooper questions the focus on fertility as the main purpose of the rite, citing a Sumerian text that suggests "the purpose of the marriage of Inanna and the king is to properly regulate relations between people, and between people and the gods."[48]

In ancient hymns that may have described the sacred marriage ritual in Uruk, Inanna and her consort Dumuzi are the prototypical couple in the rite, their courtship and marriage celebrated in Sumerian literature. The large vase from pre-Sargonic Uruk depicts a man in royal robes approaching the goddess Inanna perhaps at the door of the **gipar** (see Figure 10). Men follow him carrying baskets full of fruits and vegetables. Below these gift bearers are rows of barley and palms, rams and ewes, all tributes for the goddess. Nissen describes the sequence of figures on

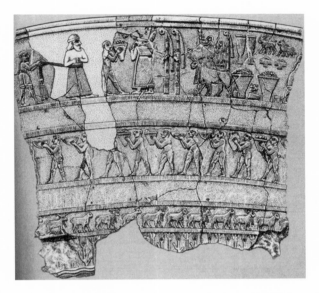

16. Reconstruction of the Warka Vase. Roaf, 1990, p. 61. Courtesy of Andromeda Oxford, Ltd.

the vase as illustrating "a world view that carefully fits man's own existence into a hierarchy by comparing him with all the surrounding phenomena."[49]

In poems of great antiquity Inanna selects Dumuzi as her consort:

> my field wants hoeing
> this is my holy word
> a dazzling palace without its sun
> I want YOU Dumuzi
> your bough raised
> Dumuzi you belong in this house
> I looked at everyone
> Dumuzi I call you
> it's you I want for prince
> *Source: tablet Ni 9602 (my transl.)*

After her selection of Dumuzi, Inanna leads him toward her sacred **gipar** for the consummation of the marriage:

she stands by the lapis door of the **gipar**
the lord goes to her
she framed in the door of heaven's storehouse
Dumuzi goes to her
tell the people to set up the bed
spread the bed with lapis grass
I want my heart's love to come in
I want my dragon of An to come in
I will place my hand in his hand
I will touch my heart to his heart
hand in my hand in blissful sleep
heart to my heart beautiful friend
it is sweet

Source: tablet TRS 70 (my transl.)

Before the consummation of the marriage, the goddess bathed. Inanna
says in one of the poems:

listen
I will scrub my skin with soap
I will rinse all over with water
I will dry myself with linen
I will spread out mighty love clothes
I know how exactly
I will look so fine
I will make you feel like a king

Source: tablet Ni 9602 (my transl.)

The king comes into the sacred bed "with lifted head" as one text says.
The marriage is consummated. In some texts the consummation is fol-
lowed by a banquet with music and festivities.

For the Sumerians the sacred union was between goddess and god,
and the human counterparts who played the role assumed divine status
during the event. Whether or not the high priestess actually engaged in
sexual intercourse and who in Ur played the part of the god Nanna in
the ritual remain controversial questions. A number of scholars concede
that the role of the high priestess in the sacred marriage is not known and
that her required chastity may have precluded her actually taking part

in the consummation of the marriage.[50] If not expected to live chastely, she may have been required to avoid pregnancy.[51]

This view is at odds with textual and historical evidence. Some en-priestesses are known to have had children. Penelope Weadock, who has written extensively on the role of the high priestess at Ur, says:

A hitherto untranslated text which is discussed by T. Jacobsen sheds consider-able light on this festival. The text tells of the gods' reward to Ur-Nammu for his piety; they ensure his royal line by giving him a son, born of the *entu*-priestess of Nanna in Nippur and presumably conceived at the time of the celebration of the sacred marriage in Nippur. Since the king took part in the ritual of the sacred marriage as Nanna in Nippur and as the *en* in Uruk, it is reasonable to believe that he also took the role of Nanna in the rite in Ur. Further, this text gives substance to the assumption that the sacred marriage was actual rather than symbolic, and at the same time it effectively controverts the suggestion that the *entu* belonged to a class of women who had to remain childless.[52]

Hall reports that in one hymn, the king puts on linen garments and lies down on a bed in the **gipar**, "an allusion to some sort of cultic ritual." [53] Another hymn says, "The En-priestess from what he had laid in her womb, bore a trustworthy man." [54]

The assumption that the Ur high priestesses were required to prac-tice chastity avoids the difficult problem of identifying the human man who took the part of the god. In the instances in which his identity is known in other cities, he is always the king. Since the high priestess at Ur was the daughter or sister (or aunt, as with Enheduanna and her nephew Naram-Sin) of the king, she would meet her father or brother or nephew at the door to the **gipar**. While it is difficult for us to imagine this incestuous union, the god-like king and the near-divine high priest-ess may have lived out a privilege only their status allowed. On the other hand, Hall states that "it is a well-attested fact that the En-priestesses of Ur were the daughters of the kings; and there is no evidence that in-cest between father and daughter to produce the heir to the throne was ever practiced in Sumer." [55] For the Mesopotamians, the ritual was a cen-tral observance that held and contained the divine mystery, the union of opposites of female and male. This sacred union of the gods was essen-tial for the fecundity of the material world. The title "sacred marriage" is not a Sumerian term; rather, it is derived from the Greek *hieros gamos*.

Similar rituals in other cultures generally fit the description of a divine marriage, or a union of the worshiper with the divine. Symbolically, the meaning and purpose of the sacred marriage reverberates on many levels, from the most elemental physical to the mystical and divine.

Examining the ritual of the sacred marriage as described by Douglas Frayne, we find elements strikingly similar to records of the ritual in-auguration of the high priestesses.[56] In turn, many of these same elements are found all over the world in rites celebrating a young woman's first menstruation or menarche.

In the inauguration ritual the high priestess is chosen by divination, the reading of the intricate markings on a sheep's liver, or by the reading of the configuration of drops of oil on water. After her selection, the chosen high priestess was anointed in the temple. Then on succeeding days her hair was ritually combed, her red garment consecrated and placed in the house of her father where she performed various sacrifices and cere-monies. In the evenings she sat on a throne and received presents: special earrings, bracelets, a red turban, a breastplate. On the sixth day the high priestess ate and left her house accompanied by "bridesmaids," her head covered like a bride. In the evening at the temple she ate a ritual meal, then received a new garment, a bed, a chair, and a stool from the elders. A special coverlet was spread over her bed. While singers chanted, the sister of the high priestess bathed her feet. The chosen priestess then lay down on the bed.

In the sacred marriage ritual, the high priestess prepared herself by ritual washing. Then, finely dressed, she waited for the god-king on a bed spread with a special coverlet. Elements similar to those associated with the inauguration include the setting up of a throne and bed, the ritual washing, the spreading of a coverlet, the gathering of ritual ob-jects, and finally, the lying down on the bed. In the sacred marriage, the king leads a procession to the door of the sacred room where the high priestess waits. After their meeting and joining, the two celebrate with a festive banquet.

In menarche rituals reported by Grahn, the young girl's feet must not touch the ground; but like the high priestess, she must sit on a special chair or throne. She must not touch her hair, so others tend it. She wears a ritual garment, red being the color that signals her highly charged status while bleeding. Her glance is considered especially potent at this time; therefore her eyes must be hidden or veiled. When she goes out,

she is accompanied by others, young friends who tend her like brides-
maids. Her feet especially are protected and washed. Her sister, who has
been on the same path before, joins in initiating her into the blood rites
of women.[57]

Based on anthropological evidence, Grahn believes the purpose of
menstrual ritual was to contain the powerful opposites of creation and
destruction. The parallels between the sacred marriage, the inaugura-
tion, and the menarche rituals suggest an inherited pattern of meaning.
Traces of ancestral memory link all these rites: treatment of the initiate
in each case is similar. The inauguration singles out the high priestess
who must enclose within the safety of the temple the clash of opposing
forces and maintain their balance. This responsibility, once shared by all
women in menstrual ritual, now was bestowed upon a single exemplary
individual. The priestess had to maintain a harmonious balance of con-
flicting life forces for all of society. This role was renewed each year with
the ritual of the sacred marriage.

The **Gipar**

Enheduanna's quarters in the building known as the **gipar** included her
private residence, and also the Ningal temple. The proximity of Ningal's
temple to her living space underscores Enheduanna's identity as "wife
of Nanna."

The original meaning of **gipar** in Sumerian is "storehouse," that is, the
structure that contains the harvest.[58] Many early carvings of a reed store-
house picture calves leaping out its doors and windows, greeting their
home-coming mothers. Inanna's stately looped reed-posts emerge from
the top of the hut (see Figure 11). Hallo and van Dijk say, "The graphic
representation of the holy stall . . . with the symbol of Inanna belongs
to the oldest Sumerian pictorial repertoire." [59] The original stall housed
young animals as well as grain from the harvest. It probably was also a
birthing hut, as Hallo and van Dijk contend: "This sacred stall may even
have served as a kind of 'lying-in hospital' for women." [60] Thus the proto-
type of the later sacred **gipar** was the central structure that contained the
fruits of an abundant yield, both animal and grain. As mistress of the
gipar, Enheduanna represents both the abundance and the preservation
of the harvest, whose success was celebrated in the ritual of the sacred
marriage.

17. Leonard Woolley's photograph of Iraqi women in the kitchen area of the gipar. *Courtesy of the Trustees of the British Museum, Negative 1044961.*

The inception of the **gipar** goes back to the origins of the reed storehouse. The structure Woolley discovered in Ur dates to Early Dynastic III, 2650–2300 B.C.E. However, earlier layers beneath this **gipar** were not excavated. The ED III structure was not reconstructed until the Ur III period (2100 B.C.E.). Enheduanna must have lived in the earliest structure Woolley discovered. The last **gipar** in the Ur series was rebuilt by the king Nabonidus for his daughter, the en-priestess Ennigaldi-Nanna, in Neo-Babylonian times around 590 B.C.E., testimony to the longevity of this tradition.

Inside the structure of the **gipar**, the high priestess was within a sacred space. In the foyer of Enheduanna's quarters was a ritual washing-place for her "private cultic use."[61] Nearby was a small sanctuary that may have been dedicated to the king, within which the high priestess prayed for his life and prosperity. In another section, a large room with a sunken waterproof floor was used for ritual cleansing. Next to it was a room with a large clay brazier. These adjacent rooms add a sense of place to Enheduanna's poetic lines:

I have heaped up coals in the brazier
I have washed in the sacred basin.

One section of the **gipar** was used as a common kitchen where meals for the gods as well as for the human occupants were prepared. In the kitchen courtyard, the excavators found a brick-lined well and a hook to anchor the well bucket. Inside the kitchen itself was a ringed hearth large enough for a "great cauldron for heating water," a grinding stone, "a table of baked brick covered with bitumen, the surface cut and scratched, apparently used to cut up meat," a round bread oven, and the base of a huge double oven, the main cooking range.[62] In these centrally placed rooms, the kitchen servants cooked and served the ceremonial meals for the gods, and daily meals for Enheduanna and her entourage.

The **gipar** was essentially a place for women. Its principal occupants were the moon goddess Ningal and the en-priestess who so intimately assumed the goddess's role on earth. All the activity in the **gipar** focused on maintaining the link between these two.

Enheduanna as Dream Interpreter

Another primary function of the high priestess was as a conduit of messages from the gods. At night the high priestess received in her sleep what Enheduanna called "Ningal's gift of dreams." She then interpreted how they pertained to individuals or to the people as a whole. In Sumer, oracular dreams had long been important messengers from the divine. A sacred marriage text describes Inanna's being asked to lie down and sleep before Dumuzi's personal god, "perhaps to obtain a dream message."[63] One scholar states that textual references "to recumbent postures are, aside from *hieros gamos* (sacred marriage), exclusively associated with dreams."[64] Hallo and van Dijk say, "Ningal, like some other goddesses, is known as a patroness of dream interpretation, and the mention of the ritual couch (literally 'fruitful, shining couch') suggests an incubation technique for eliciting the divine response."[65] In that tradition, Enheduanna continued to unravel the prophecy of dreams Ningal sent her. "While there are no exact parallels to the high priestess serving in this connection," Hallo and van Dijk assert, "it is at least worth noting the relatively large role that dream interpretation played in the attested examples of Sumerian divination, compared to its relatively modest role in the vast repertoire of later mantic techniques."[66]

The moon goddess Ningal was the daughter of Ningikuga, a reed goddess, and Enki, the god of wisdom and the sweet waters. Jacobsen believes Ningal may also have been a reed goddess.[67] In any case, with that parentage Ningal would be at home among the reeds at the edge of the marshes lining the two great rivers, the Tigris and Euphrates. Reeds fill the delta where the rivers come together at the Persian Gulf. This watery abode suits her well to become the goddess who sends gifts of dreams. In her poem of exile Enheduanna laments:

> I cannot stretch my hands
> from the pure sacred bed
> I cannot unravel
> Ningal's gifts of dreams
> to anyone

Ningal, whose name means "great lady," wanders in that borderland between dry ground and the watery deep of the rivers or ocean. In that transitional space between solid consciousness and the muddy unconscious, dreams emerge. Ningal is the divine dream-spinner who roams the marsh in the moonlight of her husband, Nanna, and taps the fertile, imaginative play of figures in the darkness that make up dreams. These she sends to her high priestess, who through training and talent interprets them.

Enheduanna's Place in History

The example set by Enheduanna influenced the tradition of the high priestess at Ur for the ensuing five hundred-year period during which successive kings appointed their daughters or sisters to the office. She began a tradition that elevated the office to a more exalted stature: "so important and sacred was the dignity of these priestesses at Ur that they were often able to retain their office undisturbed by dynastic changes in the civil government of the city."[68] Enheduanna herself attained "virtual apotheosis in the later theology."[69] She and the other en-priestesses were buried in a special cemetery beside the **gipar** at Ur. This special status of the en-priestesses even after death apparently existed early in Sumerian history. Texts refer to "certain festivals" dedicated to "the resting ones," and other records indicate that offerings of cheese, butter, dates, and oil were made to the dead en-priestesses.[70] Some were worshiped in small shrines within the Ningal temple.[71] Three hundred years after Enheduanna's death, another high priestess, Enanedu, restored the cemetery and left this dedication:

At that time, as for the 'dining room in which the *urinnu*-symbols are set up,' the place of the 'fateful day' of the ancient *entus*, the wall did not reach around its site. The breach in it was left pierced, as a wilderness; no watch was set; its site was not cleaned. I, in my great knowledge, sought room for present and future fates (i.e., deaths). I verily established a broad sacred area larger than the resting place of the old *entus;* its ruined site I verily surrounded with a great wall, a strong watch I set there, and its site I verily purified.[72]

Enanedu's dedication confirms that the high priestesses before her were held in high regard.

Enheduanna's poetry and hymns became part of the first canon of Sumerian literature adopted in the scribal schools in the temples in neo-Sumerian times (2200–1900 B.C.E.). Thanks to the neo-Sumerian apprentice scribes and the later, Old Babylonian scribal school students who copied her work as they learned their craft, several copies of Enheduanna's writings did survive. It is a small miracle that the work of this remarkable woman, buried for four thousand years, has now come to us through the efforts of archaeologists and cuneiform scholars.

CHAPTER

7

◣◢

The Poems and Hymns
of Enheduanna

We would know virtually nothing about Enheduanna were it not for her writings. She would be merely a name on a list of high priestesses at Ur, like the other daughters of the kings who held that position for five hundred years. In the treasure hunt of archaeology, finding three long poems to Inanna, three poems to Nanna, and forty-two hymns by one author is a gold mine of artistic information. Tikva Frymer-Kensky calls Enheduanna "the Shakespeare of ancient Sumerian literature in that her beautiful compositions were studied, copied, and recited for more than half a millennium after her death."[1] Texts from the Sargonic era are the first literature that can be read with fluency. Enheduanna's work was among these early compositions, and therefore her poems and hymns are part of the first known literary texts of history.

Writing had been in use in Sumer for some six hundred years before two significant changes opened the way for written language to begin to express the nuances of the spoken language. Prior to these innovations, the texts tended to consist simply of nouns strung together. The first of these changes allowed the Sumerian cuneiform signs, that normally expressed whole words, to be used to designate syllables, thus vastly expanding the number of spoken words that could be written. This added range of expression gradually led to the second change, the use of certain signs to express grammatical elements such as verb tense and person. Both innovations facilitated the process of developing a useful written vocabulary. A large library of texts that reflect these changes came from Abu Salabikh, a small town north of Nippur. Here were found the first literary texts, dated around 2500 B.C.E., including "magical incantations, hymns to temples, myths about the gods, 'wisdom' literature" — the early hymns referred to are precursors of the temple hymns of Enheduanna some two hundred years later.[2]

Enheduanna's legacy goes beyond her being the first author of record. She was a literary genius who influenced not only the function of the office of the en-priestess at Ur, but also Sumerian theology and, in present-day terms, the psychology of her time and generations afterwards. Hall calls her "the most prominent individual of this period and perhaps of any period in the history of the cult of the moon-god at Ur."[3] Most of her work survives in copies made in the Old Babylonian period, some five hundred years after her death. Her immense popularity is attested by the number of extant copies of the hymn called the "Exaltation of Inanna"; almost fifty texts have been found. Hallo and van Dijk say, "her poetic efforts must have served as a model for much subsequent hymnography."[4]

The Temple Hymns

While Enheduanna's three devotional poems to Inanna are the focus of this book, her corpus of temple hymns must not be overlooked. These

18. Table showing development of cuneiform script. Roaf, 1990, p. 70. Courtesy of Andromeda Oxford, Ltd.

PICTOGRAPHIC SIGN c. 3100 BC									
INTERPRETATION	star	?sun over horizon	?stream	ear of barley	bull's head	bowl	head + bowl	lower leg	?shrouded body
CUNEIFORM SIGN c. 2400 BC									
CUNEIFORM SIGN c. 700 BC (turned through 90°)									
PHONETIC VALUE*	dingir, an	u_4, ud	a	še	gu_4	nig_2, ninda	ku_2	du, gin, gub	lu_2
MEANING	god, sky	day, sun	water, seed, son	barley	ox	food, bread	to eat	to walk, to stand	man

* Some signs have more than one phonetic value and some sounds are represented by more than one sign. U_4 means the fourth sign with the phonetic value u.

forty-two hymns not only underscore the creative artistry of Enhedu-
anna the poet, they also present intriguing examples of ritual practice,
of the Sumerian conception of the individual goddesses and gods, and
of the theology of ancient Mesopotamia.

Each hymn is written not to the goddess or the god of the temple,
but to the holy house itself, the é, or é-gal, where the deity lived. In
the Temple Hymns the house, i.e., the temple, is variously praised as
"a watery shrine," "great lion of the wildlands," "power-gatherer of
heaven," "crown of the high plain," "wild cow," "navel of earth and
heaven." In one hymn, Enheduanna describes the Ebabbar Temple of the
sun god Utu:

> your shining horns   silver and lapis lazuli
> your lustrous lapis beard
> hangs down in profusion

Each hymn ends with this colophon:

> (name of deity) has built his/her house on your radiant site
> and placed his/her seat upon your dais

Only the final hymn, number forty-two, excludes the two lines and ends
with this colophon:

> The person who bound (this) tablet together
>   is Enheduanna
> my king
>   the thing not having been born
>   did not this one give birth to it?[5]

Since almost all existing copies of the hymns come from the Old Baby-
lonian period, four hundred to five hundred years after Enheduanna's
death, their authenticity naturally comes into question. However, ex-
cluding some obvious exceptions, such as Temple Hymn [TH] 9 to the
deified Ur III king Šulgi, scholars generally agree that the hymns origi-
nated in the Akkad period and that many, if not all, are Enheduanna's
compositions.[6] The "Temple Hymns" became part of the Old Babylo-
nian literary canon and appear in three "literary catalogues."[7] Hall says,

". . . she left to posterity a legacy of hymnic literature that became part of the fixed canon of later scribal tradition and attests to her profound impact on the Mesopotamian religious heritage."[8]

We do not know how the hymns may have been used in the temples or in the society in general. Some parts of the liturgy were apparently sung. We can imagine that the en-priestess traveled to the cities where the various temples were located and presented each hymn in some public ritualistic manner.

The temples to which the hymns are dedicated were situated in cities scattered throughout the southern Mesopotamian plain. Åke Sjöberg, whose translation of the hymns is the major scholarly redaction, locates the cities "from Eridu in the south to Sippur in the north (TH 38), and Ešunna (TH 34) to the East of the Tigris."[9] All the major temples of the time are included. The content and the geographical location of the sites "reveal best the extent of her schooling in the religious traditions of Mesopotamia," says Hall, "and her familiarity with the major deities of the Sumerian pantheon and their cult centers."[10] Some thirty-seven texts and fragmentary tablets containing the hymns remain. Three of these were found at Ur and the remainder at Nippur. Only two texts are from the Ur III period (2000 B.C.E.); the others are Old Babylonian (1900–1600 B.C.E.).

Enheduanna's compilation of the hymns may have been politically motivated. As previously noted, Sargon and his successors were plagued by the rebellious discontent of the southern Sumerian cities against the central Akkadian rule. The Temple Hymn collection, say Hallo and van Dijk, "is unique in linking the temples and cult centers of Akkad with those of Sumer."[11] Enheduanna explicitly dedicates the hymns to **lugal-mu**, "my king."

Some phrases from the hymns are striking in their woman-centeredness. Whether this is because Enheduanna was a woman, or because the culture, by virtue of its spiritual closeness to the earth and its processes—traditionally the goddess's realm—simply incorporated a more female sensibility, we cannot know. Images of female power are so uncommon in religious texts that they demand explanation, while this imagery may have been a natural element in a culture with female figures of the deity. In TH 6 to the temple of the goddess Shuzianna, for example, the poet writes:

she sows flowers in profusion
on your luminous site . . .
the lofty closed house for consecrated women

In the hymn to Ninhursag, the primary mother goddess in Sumer, she says of the temple, "your inside is a womb dark and deep." She describes in TH 15 the god Gishbanda's temple:

a mother's breast   frightening and red place
secured in the dark womb

Enheduanna's hymn number 8 to Nanna's temple at Ur, the Ekishnugal, is particularly interesting because of her residence in the **gipar** which is mentioned in the hymn. Here it is in its entirety.

O Ur
    breed bulls standing
    in the watery reed brake
white stone Ekishnugal
    calf of a great cow
    grain-eater of holy heaven
Wild Cow   a snare sprawled over a nest
Ur   first-fruit-eater of all lands
shrine in a pure place
An's first piece of earth
O house of Suen
    "princely" fits your front side
    "kingly" suits your back
your feast is an **ada** hymn
holy drums metal **ub** and leather-covered **ala**
fill your banquet
your emanating light
your faithful lordship
(are) precious things

(in) the **gipar**   the priestess' rooms
    that princely shrine of holy cosmic order
they track the passage of the moon

waning moonlight spreads over the homeland
the sweeping light of noon fills every country

O house   your shining face is
the great snake of the reed marsh
your foundation   O shrine
 the fifty **absues**
 the seven seas
has plumbed the inner-workings of the gods
your prince
 decision maker
 crown of wide heaven
he   Ashimbabbar
king of heaven   O Ur shrine
has built this house on your radiant site
and placed his seat upon your dais

The forty-two hymns are an indication of Enheduanna's stature and importance in many cities besides Ur, where she lived, and near-by Uruk, where she may have served as high priestess.[12] The theme of her hymns is one of cultural unity, and Enheduanna's inclusion of all the major temples substantiates her political role. Scholars Hallo and van Dijk sum up the hymns:

The temple hymns show us Enheduanna as a kind of systematic theologian, well versed in the subtleties of a—perhaps already traditional—set of Sumerian beliefs, and capable of adapting them to a new point of view.[13]

The Inanna Hymns

The three poems included in this book differ from the "Temple Hymns." Each one is an extended narrative praising Enheduanna's personal goddess Inanna. In these works she created a role for Inanna never before explicitly stated. While Inanna had been the subject of older myths, such as "Inanna's Descent to the Underworld," and of songs, like those in the sacred marriage literature, Enheduanna altered the traditional shape of Sumerian religious hierarchy in her poems by elevating Inanna above all other gods.

In order to understand the Inanna hymns in context, we must examine the developments taking place in the culture of the time. While cultural changes in the several hundred years prior to Sargon's takeover proceeded in an organic manner from the Sumerian base, the changes ushered in by the Akkad Dynasty, Nissen says, "were apparent in more than one sphere, so we may speak with some justification of a break with the past." [14] These changes were particularly evident in the graphic art.

Instead of clumsy, ill-proportioned human figures in art, slim, well-proportioned forms are depicted that display anatomical details. In place of the inhibition about leaving even the smallest portion of the surface area of a picture empty, we now find the intentional inclusion of empty background as a part of the composition. In place of a paratactic ordering of the elements in larger compositions, an attempt was now made to represent the relationships between the characters pictorially.[15]

Enheduanna's writings illustrated the profound changes taking place in human understanding. Somewhere between the five hundred years of Sumerian domination in the Early Dynastic period prior to Sargon and the subsequent Sargonic Age, a fundamental shift in the perception of the gods transpired. Enheduanna grew to maturity in the culture that gave rise to this new perception, and her writings articulate what formerly could only be surmised from art works. Pictorial evidence shows the gods in Enheduanna's time in more flexible, vulnerable positions vis-a-vis one another. No longer shown in stiff, traditional poses, frequently they are depicted fighting with one another. Now the gods have become individuals and vie for dominance. Their former hierarchy is no longer fixed. Nissen says these depictions "seem inconceivable without a fundamental change in the conception of the gods. It is a new way of looking at the world of the gods: one that dissolves the earlier unity of the gods as all-embracing city gods, but who could also be given special characteristics, into gods with individual responsibilities and hierarchies." [16]

Not only are the gods pictured as individuals, but their human supplicants approach them one-on-one. Often a worshiper is depicted being led by a lesser god toward a higher one. That an individual's personal god could present his/her prayers to a second god, whose power and dominion covered the particular content of the appeal, is our first historical evidence of divine intercession. Enheduanna's poem of exile is one

19. Victory stele of Naram-Sin, reddish sandstone, Susa, Akkadian Period. Courtesy of the Louvre Museum, © photo R. M. N.—H. Lewandowski.

such example of a prayer of intercession; here she begs Inanna to plead with An.

> speak to An
> he will free me
> tell him "Now"
> he will release me

20. A goddess presents a worshiper to Inanna. Left, cylinder seal; right, seal impression on clay. C. 2112–2004 B.C.E. Courtesy of the Bible Lands Museum, Jerusalem.

The image of a goddess or a god taking a person's hand that appears in many cylinder seal carvings from this era conveys the notion, heretofore unknown, of an individual's personal relationship to a deity. The world is altered by this new recognition of the value of the individual human being. Nissen says,

This clearly bears witness to a totally new independent concept of art. On the whole, we may say that this new way of seeing, this emergence of the individual, clearly reflects a change in consciousness, in which the independence and personal responsibility of the individual are for the first time given pictorial expression.[17]

In these scenes and in Enheduanna's writing, we witness that moment when an individual is selected out of the mass of humanity into a new consciousness of self-definition and self-worth. Through her relationship to Inanna, Enheduanna was able to discover her own individuality by exploring the realms of the human psyche and its unconscious matrix. Enheduanna's poetry portrays a woman deeply aware of her inner life in all its uniqueness.

Two developments begin to happen in her poetry. Enheduanna begins, first of all, to piece together a multitude of images of Inanna. Some clearly are informed by earlier tradition, and others come from the reservoir of Enheduanna's own imagination. Whatever the source, Enheduanna draws a complex picture of Inanna that probably had never been articulated before. Secondly, Enheduanna begins to understand emotion as the graze of the goddess's hand across a person's soul. Image and emotion become the language of the goddess to the particular individual. Enheduanna understood this language. Image and emotion associated with Inanna became the building blocks of her poetry. This first instance of an individual articulating her inner life in a diary-like narrative represents a profound innovation in human consciousness. No less brilliant is Enheduanna's unique interaction with Inanna, as involved and essential to her being as any subsequent mystic's description.

Enheduanna knew that the power of these unseen forces of emotion and image was real, ever present, and actively involved in shaping individual human lives. Much of Enheduanna's poetry described Inanna as she played the many parts of the emotion-laden forces in the psyche. In her description of that enigmatic and paradoxical being she called Inanna, she brought together her sense of these forces' power and her interpretation of their meaning. Not only did she feel herself buffeted by them, but she also remained certain that within the storm, the paradoxical Inanna was constantly carving out the meaning and purpose of Enheduanna's earthly life. No matter how harsh the trials inflicted upon her, Enheduanna remained inextricably bound to her goddess as the divine image that held her reason for being. This faith is at the heart of her writing.

In a particularly intimate section of the poem "The Exaltation of Inanna," Enheduanna expresses her devotion:

> child of yours   I am a captive
> bride of yours   I am a captive
> it is for my sake your anger fumes
> your heart finds no relief

Enheduanna sees the events in her life and the temper of her emotions to be intimately connected to Inanna. This verse, written in exile, eloquently states how she feels about Inanna and how Inanna feels about her. Enheduanna rests in Inanna as a child rests in her mother. Inanna protects her and loves her with a mother's love. Not only is she Inanna's child, but she is also Inanna's bride. She is married to Inanna, is her fresh, young bride who pours upon Inanna the devotion and the passion of committed love. In return, Inanna's heart finds no relief when her priestess is suffering. Inanna's anger fumes because Enheduanna is a captive in the wilderness. Their relationship is intimate, mutual, intertwined so completely that what one woman does reverberates in the other.

The passion and ardor between the high priestess and the goddess is striking. Inanna is as real to Enheduanna as a lover. The same epithet "spouse of Inanna" was used by kings to legitimize their rule at the dawn of history. Enheduanna appropriated this metaphor for herself in a woman-to-woman marriage.

The intimacy between the goddess and the high priestess does not diminish Enheduanna's understanding of Inanna as a majestic deity. Enheduanna tells us that Inanna, Queen of Heaven and Earth, is the axis around which the universe spins. Her great arms stretch out to encompass all of life. "She wears the carved-out ground plan of heaven and earth," we hear in one of the poems. She possesses the very design of life and controls the movement of the natural world. She is the transcendent sentient being who surges through matter. As such, she carries out her plan in the repetitive cycles of nature.

For Enheduanna, Inanna is the mystery behind the created world, if not the creatrix herself. Then Enheduanna goes one step further. She experiences Inanna by her side. This goddess in her wisdom chose Enheduanna to be high priestess on earth just as, according to Enheduanna, Inanna is high priestess in heaven. Enheduanna plays the part of Inanna as an earthly human being while the goddess intimately directs the course of Enheduanna's life.

Enheduanna both submits to Inanna and attempts to change her. Enheduanna completely accepts the given order of the universe as part of Inanna's divine plan. In "Lady of Largest Heart," Enheduanna draws a vivid picture of Inanna, weighing heavily the dark, destructive, bloodthirsty elements in her powers. None of this turns Enheduanna away. All the elements belong.

Within this reality is the second element of the design, Enheduanna's relationship to Inanna's plan of order. Enheduanna belongs to, interacts with, and actually influences the demanding needs of her goddess. Inanna represents a much larger reality by which Enheduanna carefully measures her daily life, but Inanna's size and power do not prevent Enheduanna from questioning and cajoling her goddess.

The Inanna poems express a theology of immanence and transcendence that already may have been a part of Sumerian religion, but Enheduanna's articulation was surely a profound and influential statement, based as it was on her own intimate history. The passion and intensity expressed in the poems could only come from Enheduanna's personal experience. She clearly sees herself, her destiny and fate, as subject to the goddess's grand design. Whatever happens to her, from her selection as High Priestess, to her exile, to the vicissitudes of her emotions, happens inside the web Inanna has spun. Inanna is the omnipotent agent of the mystery of human destiny. In spite of this omnipotence, Enheduanna, the devotee, has the power to "cool" Inanna's troubled heart. The passion of her devotion is explicitly expressed in the poems for that purpose. "I am yours / why do you slay me?" she writes in "Lady of Largest Heart." In the same poem she says with exasperation:

> stop I say
> enough
> moaning   unending lamenting
> do not cool you down
> Beloved Lady of Holy An
> look at your tormenting emotions
> all the time weeping

While Inanna is omnipotent and sometimes remote and seemingly indifferent, she, the goddess, could be moved by her devotee's pleading. The gods are not immoveable; they suffer, and they can change in response to human pleading. In "The Exaltation" Inanna "receives her prayer."

> the holy heart
> of Inanna
> returns to her

Enheduanna is restored to her rightful place in the temple through Inanna's intercession.

The Inanna poems give us a glimpse into the intimate life of an unusual woman. Added to the unique value of this fact alone, is the possibility that Enheduanna's writing records the birth of individual consciousness. Inside that consciousness, her poetry reveals the intense struggle of one woman as she confronts her destiny, the inner emotional upheaval, and the demanding outer events that make up her life.

PART

I I

The Three

Inanna Poems

Introduction

The second section of this book contains the three known poems of Enheduanna written to her personal goddess Inanna. Each poem has a brief introduction, and following each is a synopsis of its content as well as an essay on its meaning and relevance today.

Four millennia have passed since Enheduanna wrote these poems. The poet combines descriptions of the goddess's delicacy and beauty with themes of Inanna's violence and blatant power. The contrast is shocking. The mind's eye is not used to gory scenes of murder and destruction perpetrated by a goddess. We can hardly conceive of a goddess of such bloody intent. Inanna is appallingly vicious in her assaults and unrelenting in her demands.

Enheduanna was an insightful, passionate poet who lived on the cusp of an enormous cultural shift. Behind her were successive cultures that for thousands of years had understood themselves to be held in the cosmic matrix of a fecund goddess mother and her sisters. The Neolithic goddesses of Mesopotamia expressed the experience of the sacred in a variety of ways. Some, as in Jarmo and Halaf, are rotund vessels of fertility. In contrast, the Samarran goddess seems to dance with her totem scorpion to an instinctual rhythm of wild nature. The snake-headed goddess of the Ubaid culture elevates snake energy, that earth-bound creature that continuously transforms itself by shedding its skin. Probably the goddess of the animals appeared in her many forms on Halaf pottery: heron, bull, giraffe, snake. In the Neolithic period, the realm of the sacred was located in the natural world and in its ongoing processes of birth, maturation, and death.[1] While these ancestral beliefs may not have been directly subsumed into Bronze Age religion, the precept of nature's infusion with the divine was a vital assumption in Sumerian sacred literature and ritual practice. Similar beliefs formed the heart of Sumerian religion and the foundational structure within which the pantheon of Sumerian goddesses and gods were defined.

During the thousand years after Enheduanna's death, a shift in ancient Near Eastern religion took place. Male gods became more prominent in the pantheons, sometimes actually taking over the names and powers of former goddesses.[2] Eventually, out of Ur, Enheduanna's city in southern Mesopotamia, came Abraham led by Yahweh, the god of the Hebrews. Born around 1700 B.C.E., Abraham spent his early years in Ur of the Chaldees and undoubtedly spent time in the Sumerian temples with his family and young friends. Postgate tracks Abraham's journey:

Abraham moves from Ur of the Chaldees, in the far south of Sumer, up the Euphrates to Nahur, somewhere on the headwaters of the River Habur, and then southwest to Palestine, in an itinerary entirely plausible in the context of the early second millennium B.C.[3]

Whether myth or fact, accounts of Abraham's origins suggest a direct connection between Sumerian myth and religion with biblical stories and propose a source for the many biblical parallels.[4] Kramer concludes:

But there may very well have been considerable Sumerian blood in Abraham's forefathers, who lived for generations in Ur or some other Sumerian cities . . . In brief, Sumerian-Hebrew contacts may well have been more intimate than hitherto suspected, and the law which went forth from Zion (Isaiah 2:2) may have had not a few of its roots in the soil of Sumer.[5]

In the first millennium B.C.E., the Hebrew god developed a monotheistic character, although as *el\ohîm,* literally "gods," he retains his plurality.[6] This god was neither in, nor of, nature, but separate and beyond it. He is characterized by the exertion of his will, and nature responds to his command. This new consciousness of god represents a giant leap of the imagination beyond the material world. The coursing of life through matter became secondary under this god's omnipotent control; the split between nature and god was finalized.[7] Clearly a milestone in the development of consciousness, this new conception of the deity was a radical departure from the belief in the divine presence in matter.[8]

Centuries passed during which these two understandings of the divine existed side by side. Canaanite religious practices that bore a strong resemblance to those of Mesopotamia found their way into the Hebrew temples. Pillars to the goddess Ashera were erected in the sanctuary. The priestesses to the goddess actually lived in the temple. There they wove Ashera's garments, just as they had woven the garments of the moon goddess Ningal in Enheduanna's **gipar** at Ur.[9]

Enheduanna's poetry can be seen as a reassertion of the religion of "the old, old gods." Her Inanna combats any attempt to call into question the primacy of nature as the body of the goddess. In the poem "Inanna and Ebih" this conflict is explicit. An Edenic paradise on the slopes of the mountain Ebih threatens to defeat Inanna. The god of heaven, An, Inanna's great supporter, bends toward Ebih's unnatural, idealized, conflict-free world. An's seduction by Ebih anticipates Yahweh's persuasion of Adam and Eve that his garden paradise could be theirs for the price of their obedience. This garden is not the nature Inanna rules at all.

Sensing the threat from the gods who long for paradise, like An and Ebih, Enheduanna in "Inanna and Ebih" elevates Inanna above all the Sumerian gods. In the second poem, "Lady of Largest Heart," she establishes her goddess as the supreme, unequivocal expression of the reality of the cosmos. This poem is the most complete account discovered to date of the ancestral religions whose central deities were goddesses.

Enheduanna's third poem, "The Exaltation of Inanna," is a premonition of Inanna's impending defeat. In this poem Enheduanna is exiled from her place in the temple, cast into the wilderness by a usurping priest or general. While Enheduanna ultimately regains her position as high priestess, the poet accurately anticipates the overthrow of the supremacy of the goddess she had upheld.

At the beginning of a new millennium, humanity still suffers as a result of the separation of spirit from matter that took place in antiquity. Yahweh's split and Greek-influenced Christianity's additions to the separation of good and evil provide divine sanction for the dark/light oppositional mentality that pervades our psychology. Dominant monotheistic religions effectively taught generations that evil is outside ourselves, with Satan over there, in others. We learned to deny our own potential for evil.

The splitting of good and evil by the Hebrew, and the subsequent Christian, god was persuasively supported by the Greek system of logical, rational thought that eventually superseded the primacy of nature and myth. Poet Charles Olson, who translated Sumerian poetry, used Heraclitus' adage, "Man is estranged from that with which he is most familiar," to capture the essence of his thinking and to express his belief that post-modern men and women could rediscover and revitalize their connection to the natural, the most familiar.[10] He complains of, "the individual as ego . . . that peculiar presumption by which western man has interposed himself between what he is as a creature of nature (with certain instructions to carry out) and those other creations of nature. . . ."[11]

Perhaps only events as large and as abhorrent as the Holocaust and Hiroshima could jar us into recognizing the potential evil in everyone. To face the events of World War II, not to mention subsequent wars and human destruction, we must shift radically our perception of human psychology.

The separation between good and evil perpetuated by our dominant religious beliefs reflects a normal part of human psychology. Psychologists have long understood the important role projection plays in the psyche. The worldview that develops as a result of an individual's childhood circumstance continues to influence her/his perception of the environment. Motives, attitudes, and values from the past are projected onto people in the present. This psychological tendency serves as a defense against having to recognize and accept our own ignoble motives. Fortunately we also have the capacity, by means of serious psychological work, to become conscious enough to withdraw projections of our own darkness from other people, ideas, and institutions. However, this can only be carried out by strongly motivated individuals striving for greater moral and psychological integrity.

Enheduanna's poetry insists that we see fully both the magnificent and the horrendous acts of which human beings are capable. Nature, she writes, is both dark and light. Knowing this, we expect dark and light; and more importantly, we begin to recognize this polarity in ourselves. Inanna offers an exceedingly realistic picture of human nature. Only by acknowledging our capacity for evil can we possibly learn to contain it.

In my renditions of the poems, I have attempted to make readable, understandable verse without straying from the essential meaning of the original texts. While I relied on the line by line study with Daniel Foxvog, I alone am responsible for the versions of the poems. Dan Foxvog never saw the renditions as I worked on them, nor did he see the finished product. He provided me with copies of the Sumerian texts that included comments by other scholars on the meaning of various words. From these copies and from notes I took during our conversations, I rendered each line. As the poems took shape, they posed many questions and suggested various alternative readings as I describe in the upcoming chapter. Other writers have worked in this manner, rendering languages they did not know into English, including the poet Charles Olson who termed his Sumerian translations "transpositions."[12] I am exceedingly appreciative of Near Eastern scholars whose lives are spent in the pursuit of understanding ancient civilizations and their languages. I trust that this foray into their territory will serve to acquaint others with the value of their work.

The poems were originally copied in cuneiform script on wet clay tablets and preserved for millennia under the desert sand of present-day Iraq. Because Enheduanna's poems were copied in the scribal schools after her death, there are a number of exemplars of each poem. Nevertheless, many of the tablets are broken, leaving scholars a virtual puzzle to piece together. I identify places in the poems where lines are missing, indicating that the number of missing lines from the existing exemplars can be counted, but that these lines do not exist on the tablets recovered to date.

At some point in the poems, I have inserted artificial headings or marked breaks to separate sections in order to clarify meaning. I also used capital letters or italics for emphasis, a stratagem not found in the original texts. Throughout, I have used poetic license in the hope of enhancing the meaning and readability of the images. The poems are a work of the heart for this great poet, Enheduanna, and I trust their flaws will be viewed in this light.

CHAPTER

8

∧ ∕

The First Poem
Inanna and Ebih

Introduction

The poem "Inanna and Ebih" is a story of a conflict between the goddess Inanna and a defiant mountain named Ebih. Ultimately Inanna triumphs over Ebih, but in the process, the great god An, attracted by Ebih's audacious disobedience, abandons his alliance with Inanna. Traditionally An had been Inanna's key supporter and the source of her divine power; his refusal to stand by her shakes the cosmic order.

Ebih has been identified as the modern Jebel Hamrin. Postgate describes this escarpment of the Zagros as "an abrupt rock wall" that "runs in an amazingly straight and regular line for hundreds of kilometers."[1] This section of the Zagros was known as Mount Ebih from earliest times. J. V. Kinnier Wilson, in his study of this area, identified a nine mile scar in the series of broken hills that make up the Jebel Hamrin as the aftermath of an earthquake around 9500 B.C.E. Wilson presents the possibility that the Sumerians believed their gods originated in the gaseous eruptions from Mount Ebih.[2]

Strategically, the escarpment divides two important regions, the northern plains of the Zab-Dijala rivers region on the northeast and the alluvial plain of Sumer and Akkad on the southwest. So important was the region as a protection to Sumer and Akkad's peripheral flank that, as M. B. Rowton reports, "the kings of the Third Dynasty of Ur (built) a wall right across its outer fringe, all the way from the Euphrates to the point where the Dijala breaks through the Jebel Hamrin."[3] Sargon and Naram-Sin are both known to have penetrated the area, once lush with forests. Hallo and van Dijk state that the territory of Ebih revolted "presumably against Naram-Sin."[4] With Inanna/Ishtar at his side he was victorious.

While the poem may be based on an actual event, it contains elements of a mythic narrative just beneath the historical that gives the poem a more complex, more profound meaning. Behind the story lies a conflict between the most basic components of human desire, and need. Enheduanna has built this poem around the fundamental struggle in the psyche between the backward pull of the idealized world of paradisiacal bliss and the forward impetus toward states of competence, autonomy, and independence. In order for Inanna to prevail over Ebih, she has to overcome her dependence on An. The poem contains a wealth of psychological insight, striking in its anticipation of modern theories.

"Inanna and Ebih" must have been the first of the three poems of Enheduanna, because the events it describes are referred to in the next two poems. Also, the poem unequivocally establishes Inanna as foremost of all the gods. This was a necessary step in Enheduanna's attempt to strengthen the ancestral religion in the face of threats to its centrality.

Like other pieces of Mesopotamian literature, particularly the Sumerian myth of the great flood, this poem is a precursor to a biblical story. Ebih's peaceable kingdom, where fruit trees are eternally bearing and where natural enemies among animals live together in harmony, is a forerunner of the biblical Garden of Eden. More importantly, the psychology behind the Genesis story and Enheduanna's poem about Ebih are strikingly similar.

As we enter the world of "Inanna and Ebih," we encounter our own psychological heritage before it became crystallized in biblical literature. Enheduanna's heritage reaches far back before the biblical stories, back through millennia to religions and cultures based on the infusion of nature with the sacred. With Inanna's victory over Ebih, Enheduanna sought to preserve this religion.

INANNA AND EBIH

IN-NIN-ME-HUŠ-A [5]
by The Priestess Enheduanna

I. Invocation

Lady of blazing dominion
clad in dread
riding on fire-red power

Inanna
holding a pure lance
terror folds in her robes

flood-storm-hurricane adorned
she bolts out in battle
plants a standing shield on the ground

Great Lady Inanna
    battle planner
    foe smasher

you rain arrows on enemies
set strength against foreigners
lion roar across heaven
on earth bodies struck
flesh cut

wild bull
    hooves planted
    battle-ready against foe

fiery lion
    the upstart and rebel
    you persuade
    with your gall

II. Praise to Her

my Lady
    godly child   nursed in heaven

Inanna
    godly maiden   ripened on earth
YOU ARRIVE
your spread-out arms
wide as the Sun King

when you wear fearsome dread in heaven
crystal brilliance on earth

when you unfold from the mountains
your woven net of blue lapis cord[6]

when you bathe
in clear mountain streams
you, mountain born
in a crystal-pure place

when you wear
the robes
of the old, old gods

when you slice heads
like a scythe cuts wheat swaths

then the black-headed[7] praise you with song
the Sumerians sing in one voice
everyone sings sweetly a joy song

Queen of battle
    the Moon God's oldest child[8]
Maiden Inanna
I worship you
here is my song

III. Inanna Sings

I the Lady
circling the sky
circling the earth

I Inanna
circling the sky
circling the earth

in the east circling the Elam lands
in the northwest circling the Subir lands
in the north circling the Lullubi lands[9]

I ATTACK
THE MOUNTAIN
AT ITS HEART

I the Lady
came near
and the mountain did not fear

I Inanna
came near
the mountain did not fear
came near Mount Ebih
the mountain did not fear

did not tremble
of its own accord
nor wipe its nose on the ground
nor flatten its lips in the dust
I grab the upstarts in my hands
shake them
make them fear me

set a great ox
against its great strength
a calf
against its small strength

I chase them with my rope dance
goad them with my jump rope[10]
I ignite battle
        arrows quiver-ready
I braid thick rope slings
        polish wood-spear
        javelin, shield

set fires in their forest borders
        ax the wicked
call the Fire God, pure Gibil
to flame trunks and thick branches

from my own city
Aratta [11]
hidden jewel and sparkling
I spread terror all down the mountain

like an An-cursed place
never again will rise
like a ruin where Enlil frowned
never will lift its neck [12]

PRAISE MY WAY MOUNTAIN!
PRAISE ME!
PRAISE WITH SONG!

iv. Inanna Goes to An

Inanna
      child of the Moon God
a soft bud swelling [13]
her queen's robe cloaks the slender stem
on her smooth brow she paints
fire beams and fearsome glint

fastens carnelian
blood-red and glowing
around her throat

and then her hand clasps
the seven-headed mace
she stands as in youth's prime [14]
her right hand grasps the mace

steps, yes she steps her narrow foot
on the furred back   ·
of a wild lapis lazuli bull

and she goes out
white-sparked, radiant
in the dark vault of evening's sky
star-steps in the street
through the Gate of Wonder

and goes before the god
offers him the first fruits
with sacrificial prayer

An stretches out his hands
takes the fruit in
pleased, he receives Inanna

then sits in the place
he calls his own
and motions her
beside his great right hand

she speaks:
An
my father[15]
be well! **silim!** [16]
listen to my words
give me your ear

An, your word
proclaimed throughout heaven
dread of my fearsome brilliance

An, you are he who
gives my word weight
over all others
in heaven and on earth
who gives my iron cold ax
dominion to heaven's outer edge

who carved godly pillars[17]
     beautiful as queens
to mark the place I stand
there you set my solid throne
there you bent the impaling pole
to my eager hands

and I ride out
team of six in harness
pulled over sky roads
to the bounds of heaven
I come forth a queen
like cool moonlight down the breast of the sky

arrows shot from my hands
strip field, forest, orchard
like the teeth of locusts

arrows sharp as harrows
level the rebel's field

my hands like falcon claws
slash heads
like the FIRST SNAKE
I come out of the mountains[18]
fast as snakes slip through earth cracks
I smash heads

An   KING
I carry your name
unraveled on a flaxen cord
to the edge of the earth

my eyes scan the earth
I know the length of it

I travel heaven's pure road
I know the depth of it

even the holy Annuna[19]
stand in awe of me
listen!
I the Lady
came near
and the mountain did not fear

I Inanna came near
the mountain did not fear

came near
Mount Ebih
the mountain did not fear

did not tremble
of its own accord
nor wipe its nose on the ground
nor flatten its lips in the dust

I grab the upstarts in my hands
shake them
make them fear me

set a great ox
against its great strength
a calf
against its small strength

I chase them with my rope dance
goad them with my jump rope

I ignite battle
        arrows quiver-ready
I braid thick rope slings
        polish wood-spear
        javelin, shield

set fires in their forest borders
        ax the wicked
call the Fire God, pure Gibil
to flame trunks and thick branches

from my own city
Aratta
hidden jewel and sparkling
I spread terror all down the mountain

like an An-cursed place
never again will rise
like a ruin where Enlil frowned
never will lift its neck

PRAISE MY WAY MOUNTAIN!
PRAISE ME!
PRAISE MY WAY EBIH!
PRAISE WITH SONG!

An
king of the gods
answers her

Little One
my Little One

you ask for the mountain
you want the heart of it
    he says this to her
you the Queen
you ask for Mount Ebih
you want the heart of it
    he says this to her

Mount Ebih
you ask for it
you want the heart of it
    he says this to her

the gods
standing in their place
bend with fear of Ebih
the Annuna
sitting in their holy place
tremble, stricken
their flesh prickles all over

a red-hot terror
paralyzes our whole country

fiery terror of the mountain Ebih
rages in the lands around us[20]

the jagged peaks of Mount Ebih
cut the blue vault of sky
trees
fruit laden, full grown
stand luxuriant on its slopes
layers of thick leaves
on its great trees
darken the sky

lion pairs
stroll in the shade
of stretching arch of branches

grey-fleeced wild rams
wide-eyed stags

roam the hills without shepherds
wild bulls come and go
legs brushed by swaying grass

the crescent-horned ibex
mates in the mountain cypress
I am fear-struck
at their lavish brilliance
I will not go there with you

O maiden Inanna
I will not set my head with yours
against the fiery radiance of the mountain
    An says this to her

INANNA! PORTENTOUS ONE!
HOLY! ILL-BODING!
FURY OVERTURNS HER HEART!

with screech of hinge
she flings wide the gate
of the house of battle

her hands pull the bolt lock
on its lapis lazuli door

bedlam unleashed
she sends down a raging battle
hurls a storm from her wide arms
to the ground below

thin sinew the woman strings
for her flawless arrows

and hurricane winds
swift-piercing, stinging
fly with Inanna's fury
suck loosened earth into sweet air

dust chokes every blink and breath
broken bits and fiery chips
swirl in the dust dark air

my Queen batters the mountain
plants her heels hard
rubs dagger's edge on a whet stone

grabs Ebih by the neck
as she would a sheaf of rushes

in ear-splitting waves
her shrill cries pierce
Ebih's failing heart

with stones from its own slopes
she pelts   she pounds
thud dub   thud dub
storms of stones crack its sides

damp and writhing snakes
tangled in branches
drop at her drear bidding
spitting deadly venom

and her tongue's poison
hurls a green-wilting curse
over forest and fruit-bearing trees

she shows no mercy
to its green plant rows
a parching drought she blows
dust dry air in her pitiless wake
gusts over stems of verdant growth
not a moist drop stays

in the bent and withered grass
she strikes fires
flames cut the sky to the boundary stones
flames dance in the smoke stained air
spread at a glance from the queen's glare

holy Inanna
fresh faced, fearless
vigor of a young man commanding

wrestles the mountain to its knees
stands the victor at its base

MOUNTAIN!   she cries
EBIH!

because you puff yourself up
because you stand so high
dress up so beautiful
make yourself so green and luscious
put on a royal robe
stretch your hand straight to An

do not wipe your nose on the ground
do not flatten your lips in the dust
I HAVE KILLED YOU
I HAVE STRUCK YOUR HEART WITH SORROW

you thick-hided elephant
I will twist your trunk
you oversized bull
I will wrench your neck
grab your thick horns
throw you in the dust
stomp you with my hatred
grind my knees in your neck
till tears wet your face
sorrow grips your heart

turn your back on me!
may the bleak bird of heartbreak
nest in your shadows

Inanna
fearsome victor
speaks again
MOUNTAIN
father Enlil led me
placed the dreaded mace
in my strong right hand
in my left I swing an ax
mace and ax flung raging
cut like a great toothed harrow

v. Inanna Builds a Temple to Her Victory

stone upon stone
I build a temple
mark out my estate
stone upon stone
finish it in splendor
standing hard on bedrock
grand is the throne there

summon a **kurgarra** for holy office
bestow the sacred implements
hallowed mace and dagger

summon a **gala,** singer of lamentation
dispense the tools of office
kettle drum and hand drum[21]

summon holy attendants
for ritual head-overturning
priest to become woman
priestess to become man[22]

I build this splendid temple
who dared attack the mountain
who now stands victorious

a swollen spilling water
I have washed over the grasslands
a rushing risen water
I have overrun the rope fence

mountain
I have triumphed
Ebih
I have triumphed

eldest daughter of the Moon
that you destroyed Ebih
O maiden Inanna
be praised

and praise be to Nisaba
goddess of writing

"Terror Folds in her Robes"

As with any visionary, Enheduanna's insights were rooted in the culture in which she lived. This sensitive, intelligent woman had a passion for the goddess Inanna, and this passion fueled her writing. We learn from her poetry that she undertook to keep alive an ancient tradition, reaching back a thousand years or more to the beginning of the myth and story and song that surrounded the worship of Inanna. In "Inanna and Ebih" she intimates her purpose when she says of Inanna:

> you wear the robes
> of the old, old gods

In this poem, Enheduanna makes explicit the religion that Inanna embodies. Inanna's power lies in the force of nature. Natural process, with its inevitable ebb and flow, scarcity and want, growth and destruction, emanates from the hands of Inanna. In her being Inanna contains the myriad antithetical forces that make up the natural world. At her will she unleashes whatever combinations please her.

> I the Lady
> circling the sky
> circling the earth

We see Inanna as a great bird flying over her domain. When she glides over the earth, over the sky on her spread-out wings, she expects submission. Surely all creatures tremble in the shadow of her great wings passing.

Juxtaposed against Enheduanna's devotion to the sacred essence in the natural world was the seduction of acquisition and conquest that sent her father's armies into ever more distant battles. The exhilarating news of his successes must have swept through the townships like an irresistible wind. Ruling most of the known world, Sargon and his successors fed on a new dimension of energetic will that disregarded any respect for boundaries, political or cultural. Sargon followed in the footsteps of the first kings who ruled in the Early Dynastic period, five hundred years before him. One of these, Lugalannemundu, declared himself "lord of the four quarters," and controlled the entire fertile crescent around

2600 B.C.E. Enheduanna applied this epithet to Inanna in her attempt to
elevate her to the position of foremost of the gods. In the poem "Lady
of Largest Heart" she says:

> Your torch flames
> heaven's four quarters
> spreads splendid light in the dark

However loyal and devoted Enheduanna was to her father and his suc-
cessors, her two brothers and her nephew, she must have noted the oppo-
sitional pulls between this relentless quest for new territories and her
own dedication to the ebb and flow of nature. The religion she embraced
was based on the creative fecundity of great goddesses who, long before
Inanna, had been at the center of religious worship for aeons in the Neo-
lithic and the Paleolithic periods. To defy the laws of the goddesses was
unthinkable. The conquests by the Sargonic kings could easily have pre-
cipitated Enheduanna's insight that defiance of natural process threat-
ened the heart of the old religion.

In the poem "Inanna and Ebih," Enheduanna reestablishes Inanna as
queen of the intrinsic natural laws. The threat to Inanna is a defiant
mountain named Ebih who dares to subvert the goddess's longstanding
dominion. Ebih does not fear, does not tremble, does not wipe its nose on
the ground, nor flatten its lips in the dust. What audacity! She grabs the
upstart by the neck! She demands its praise! Still it will not bow down.

Enheduanna in her vision captures the essential elements of a sweep-
ing archetypal change in consciousness on the eve of its birth. On the
one hand, in keeping with the old religion, Inanna insists that nature's
cyclic laws are binding. There is no escape. In the poem she becomes the
goddess above all others who will enforce this principle.

Ebih, on the other hand, imagines a peaceable kingdom that defies the
very laws of nature. Inanna's lion, sheep, wild cattle, deer, and ibex —
that is, natural enemies — live on Ebih's grassy slopes without shepherds.
Fruit trees are ever-bearing. Nature itself has changed. Ebih has found
a secret that alters the survival plan of animals and the cyclic ebb and
flow of vegetation. Inanna's "what-had-always-been" rule no longer ap-
plies there, and Ebih swells up big as the sky with its discovery. Ebih
appears to have brought into being a situation outside the binding im-
peratives of matter. Ebih has imagined the unthinkable: the goddess and

her unalterable design in the material world can be overcome, bypassed, superseded.

This thought contained the seed of a new possibility, namely a god who could exist *outside* the laws of nature. Enheduanna was caught between two vast ages, the ancient one dominated by the feminine principle of the divine in matter and the emerging new age dominated by the masculine spirit in a god that eventually existed entirely separate from matter as a result of Greek-influenced Christianity.

For the past three thousand years, human consciousness in the western world has evolved within the governing structure of the second paradigm, the divine as separate from matter. So powerful is this invisible, basic assumption that it becomes the lens through which all life is perceived. Enheduanna's views may appear foreign and even disturbing, based as they are on ancient assumptions. We have to suspend our fundamental beliefs and drastically shift gears in our thinking in order to apprehend what she is saying.

Ebih in the poem is an idealized place imagined as blissfully free of conflict, endlessly pouring forth its bounty. Trees on its slopes are lush with fruit. Animals of all kinds feed on abundant grasses. The lion lies down with the lamb.

An's departure from Inanna is the beginning of a powerful split. Ebih and An repudiate the tension between Inanna's paradoxical cycles of dark and light, longing instead for the sweet bliss of eternal abundance. What is dark will be cast out. Like babes swaddled in the arms of the good mother, Ebih and An turn in to her breasts forever. The fateful possibility has been thought.

"I Will Not Go There With You"

In the story of Inanna and Ebih we observe the interaction of the mythological elements, An/Ebih and Inanna. An is the great god of heaven, one of the four great gods of the Sumerians. In many myths An is the god who distributes the **me** at the beginning of time, giving out these principles of order and authority to the various other gods. The **me** are the organizing principles as well as the many elements that make up society. Each of the gods was given a portion of **me** over which she or he would preside. That An had the **me** to begin with imbues him with a power beyond all others.[23]

Inanna reminds An in the poem of his original empowerment of her, which gave her "word weight / over all others / in heaven and on earth." To her "iron cold ax" he gave "dominion to heaven's outer edge." She reciprocates this grant of power by carrying his name "unraveled on a flaxen cord / to the edge of the earth." Because of An's gifts, Inanna says:

> even the holy Annuna
> council of the gods
> stand in awe of me

When Inanna prepares to go to An for help against the rebellious Ebih, she assumes their mutual relationship is firmly in place. She has no reason to believe otherwise. She is granted the favored seat by his great right hand and begins to remind him of the complementary arrangement they have had for aeons. Naturally she would come to An when a lowly mountain goes against her will.

At this point in the poem Enheduanna introduces a surprise. The authoritative, dependable An is pulled off balance by the sight he sees on the slopes of the mountain Ebih. Something turns An's head. Some news, some allure fills his eyes with wonder. The foundation of heaven and earth is shaking. Great An trembles. The flesh of the Annuna prickles. The Land is paralyzed in fiery terror. The great god is changing, lured by the seductive scene on the mountain. An is fear-struck. Ebih's daring scares An to the point of goose bumps, at the same time it rivets his gaze in fascination. He will not join Inanna in battle against the mountain.

Great An's head is turned. Ebih has accomplished what he, An, hardly dared to dream. So awed is An by Ebih that he is stricken with fear and trembles. An is intensely drawn to Ebih. Ebih gives form to a potent desire, one so forbidden that An hardly recognizes it as also his own. Instead he is awestruck and afraid, his eyes fixed on the mountain. He is paralyzed. He has been hit with the force of an unthinkable idea. This idea lay dormant, fomenting, but not expressed, then burst forth with Ebih. An was terrified to see the new idea so openly exposed: Ebih dares to defy the inescapable rule of the goddess over the dark and light cycles in the natural material world.

An's fascination cracks the very foundation of the old religion. This moment in the dramatic action of the poem reveals the critical impasse between the two gods, Inanna and An. Enheduanna's intuition of the threat to the old order dominated by the ancient religion becomes apparent. An is pulled from his commanding position by his desire for the lush and conflict-free potential he sees on Ebih. With An's refusal, Enheduanna tells us, the old order is giving way. The possibility of overcoming nature has been proposed. The archetypal basis for this enormous change is the alluring pull to the paradise-like scene on Ebih, reminiscent of the protective arms of the mother.

By placing An at the center of the change, Enheduanna implies that in the arena of the father, or father principle, revolution is stirring. Up to this time the male deities had been a part of the religion of nature. Now, out of a restlessness or an impatience with domineering nature, an idea originates that proposes, however naively, that nature can become all-giving or even controlled. Out of the masculine world of the authoritative father, namely An, the idea of altering or controlling nature's process surfaces.

"Fury Overturns Her Heart"

In Enheduanna's consciousness the goddess is far from defeated. The poem confirms Inanna's superiority. Inanna's reaction is swift and fierce. At the moment of An's refusal she rises to her full stature as ruling goddess. No longer can she look to An for support. She alone must enforce the elements of nature's cycles. She alone is in charge.

Inanna starts out in a role familiar to many modern women, that of being empowered by a father or other male figure under whose authority she operates.[24] An gave Inanna her domain, and she reveled in it. He created the pathways of her world, and she had no problem treading them. She obeys, and she is given powers. She colludes, and she shines as his helpmate. He smiles on her, makes promises.

When she is thwarted, she calls on him. She knows how to dress, how to take him gifts. So intent is she on succeeding in this world of his making that she might forget the natural bent of her will, the effortless flow of her instinct. This performance in his service becomes her master-piece. She goes to him to get what she wants. She is, as the poem says:

> Inanna
> child of the Moon God

Her lineage is already reckoned through her father, not through her mother, Ningal, as it would have been long ago. Power issues from the father. The great gods are all "fathers." The rule of the mother has already passed.

Inanna is innocent, pubescent, a soft bud swelling. She takes on queenly posture with a royal robe. She paints a fierce mask on her face, fastens the blood-red necklace, grabs the dreadful seven-headed mace. She strikes a pose, that of a young man in his prime. Even her own female strength is already named in the masculine gender.

An calls her "little one." He cuts right through the queen's robe, the fire beams, the fearsome glint, the mace. He reminds her she is young, small, a daughter to him, not much without him, dependent on his authority.

At the moment of his unresponsiveness, at the moment of his refusal to help her, Inanna swells to her full stature. Beneath the compliant daughter is the whole and sufficient goddess. Beneath the dependent maiden is the one-in-herself heiress to the ancient rulers of female pantheons. Beneath the helpmate to An is the memory of all the goddesses who had dwelt in the caves, on the mountains, and in the temples, attracting worshippers with their sacred, magnetic force. Inanna recovers her memory, recovers her will, recovers the effortless flow of her natural unconstrained self.

We witness a moment of transformation. She who formerly bowed to great An, as daughter to father, now moves on her own, against his will, to destroy Ebih. Fury overturns her heart. She swells into her full stature. Filled with ill-boding will, Inanna commands her forces, free of An, free of the Annuna, superior to all gods. Following Ebih's destruction, we see that a new Inanna reigns. She is transformed. The Queen builds a palace on the bedrock of her new status. The consciousness of the goddess presides in ritual fullness from the splendid temple. Inanna's powers are in and of herself. She rules alone, not at the behest of An.

A swollen, over-spilling river, Inanna has washed over the boundaries of the presiding order. Fences do not contain her. Whatever constrictions the father gods tried to put on her she has swept away in the flood of her primal waters. She has seized control of the effortless flow of her natural forces, overriding the constraints of limiting cultural boundaries. Inanna has regained primacy, and Enheduanna has ensconced her goddess once and for all in a position superior to An. With the triumphant success of Inanna over Ebih, Enheduanna sets the stage for the recitation of her theology in the next poem, "Lady of Largest Heart."

"Because You Puff Yourself Up . . ."

After Enheduanna's death, the superiority of her goddess was eroded bit by bit. The disregard for the fundamental primacy of nature and the increasing centrality of conquest, war, and armies in Mesopotamian culture glorified the conquering hero and diminished the role of goddesses in the pantheon. The scenario Enheduanna had fought to prevent came into being. The worshipers of Yahweh gradually eradicated all traces of the Canaanite goddesses in the Hebrew temples, erasing at the same time the worshipers' image of the divine in matter.

The story of Ebih echoes the creation accounts in the Book of Genesis. There are two accounts of creation, one in the first chapter of Genesis and one in the second and third. The account in the second chapter raises questions that pertain to the old nature religions, specifically to male reliance on the defense of controlling natural process.

In the Genesis account of the Garden of Eden the author attempts to grapple with the problem paradise poses. Like Mt. Ebih, the paradise where Yahweh places Adam and Eve is eternally abundant. Fruit trees are ever-bearing. A snag in the plan develops when Eve is drawn to the theriomorphic goddess, Snake, who, like her Neolithic snake sisters, carries the wisdom of the sacred in the natural world. Snake beckons Eve back into their ancient alliance where cyclic dark and light are held in a unifying round. Snake in this story plays the part of Inanna, the goddess who upholds the fundamental processes of the natural, material world. Biblical scholar John A. Phillips says of this part of Genesis, "Perhaps the writer meant to recall that ancient association between sacred women and serpents in religions of the Near East. Snakes were thought to control 'wisdom' (magic), immortality, and fertility."[25]

The woman Eve is drawn to the snake and her promise to bestow on Eve full knowledge of the opposites of good and evil. No longer will she live in blissful unawareness, like a babe swaddled in her mother's arms, but will know good and evil, light and dark, the full range of opposites that are the reality of the world of matter and the foundation of the religion Snake represents.

Yahweh declares Snake's world of natural process a punishment. He "strikes enmity between the woman and the snake"[26] and thus splits human consciousness from its former embeddedness in the opposites of natural cycles. He banishes the couple from their idealized garden to

21. Cylinder seal of Inanna, bare-legged, with her foot on a lion. The bare-legged posture is very unusual in the art of this period. Courtesy of the Oriental Institute of the University of Chicago.

suffer forever the harsh penalty of the real world. The Goddess and her sacred realm of nature are now a punishment, while Yahweh is the new object of worship.

The poem "Inanna and Ebih" is the first account of an attempt to elude the laws of the goddess's inescapable cycles. It records the beginnings of a profound archetypal shift in human consciousness away from the goddess's intrinsic existence inside nature toward a male god of the spirit, completely separate and distinct from nature.

In the Genesis account, Eve eats the apple of full conscious awareness. Adam, who joins her in the feast, immediately becomes aware of his sexuality, of their gender difference, of the contrasts inherent in the created world. For Inanna, this world of contrasts is the sacred realm in which human beings must bend pride and will in the face of the goddess's inevitable boundaries. For Yahweh, the natural world is a punishment, while the world of merged bliss in the Garden is paradise.

Yahweh warned the couple that if they eat from the tree of knowledge, they will die, a strong admonition against gaining consciousness. Snake, Eve's natural archetypal wisdom, reveals Yahweh's deceit. Indeed, the couple would not die, but would wake up to the facts of the real world. Yahweh appears to have a bias for paradise and for the unconscious bliss of merging with the all-giving mother. He does not want his son, Adam, whom he created first and to whom he gave special powers, to suffer the sacrifice and pain of full masculine development. Yahweh's bias is consistent with the difficult pulls men endure psychologically between longing for the protection of the mother versus embarking on the road of phallic assertion and independence.

Is Yahweh's declaration that Adam will dominate his wife Eve compensation for her disobedience? Or is it possible that Adam could not tolerate her full equality? At a similar point in the Ebih story, An displays his bias for paradise, upon which Inanna rises to assert her full equality with him. An disappears from the story in the face of Inanna's fury. Heels planted, hands on hips, she rebukes the defeated mountain for its arrogance. The mountain was puffed up. The mountain stood too high. The mountain was inflated, arrogant, elevated above the leveling realities of fate, suffering, and death. The mountain tried to reach its hand to the transfixed An, bypassing Inanna altogether. She will not allow it.

Yahweh obligingly orders Eve's submission.[27] The suspicion that Adam could not tolerate Eve's equality is borne out in an ancient Hebrew legend. According to this story, Adam had a wife before Eve named Lilith, a woman who demanded equality. She refused to lie beneath Adam in sexual intercourse. "Why must I lie beneath you?" she asked. "I also was made from dust, and am therefore your equal."[28] Because Adam tried to compel her obedience by force, Lilith in a rage uttered the "ineffable name of God, rose in the air and left him."[29] Lilith escaped to the Red Sea where God punished her by killing one hundred of her demon children every day.[30]

The banished Lilith carried with her women's fierce independence, sexual passion and initiative, and mysterious knowing through the body. These characteristics, natural potentials of most women, were split off from the woman who became idealized by men, the obedient wife and mother, Eve. **Lil**, a destructive storm or wind spirit from Sumer, from whom Lilith derives her name, has characteristics parallel to Inanna's: as a wind spirit, she hurls storms, biting dust, hurricanes. In the contrast between Lilith and Eve, we see that the fierce, raging Inanna of the death powers, the erotic Inanna, even the Inanna who takes initiative in the creation of cultural forms in a fully independent way, is banished to the Red

Sea in the form of Lilith. Eve, who remains, is destined to be obedient to her husband, to lie beneath him, and to give birth in pain.[31] Any remnant of the Inanna of Enheduanna's poems is obscured in the constrained, humiliated Eve. In spite of this god's dictum, women continued to worship "the queen of heaven" even into the time of the prophet Jeremiah. "Behold, my anger and my wrath will be poured out on this place," he says (7:20, RSV). Stirring his wrath were the women who "knead dough, to make cakes for the queen of heaven" (7:18). Some say the cakes were crescent-shaped replicas of the new moon.

Yahweh and his earthly servant, Adam, collude to limit women's expression of the full range of their being. This limitation obviously affects men as well. With the containment of Eve's sexuality, the possibility of unbridled erotic exploration is gone, a loss to both. Gone, also, is the possibility of mutual esteem for creative efforts, for Eve is subordinate to her husband. The Adam who remains is artificially empowered by the massive repression of Eve's natural emotions and the denial of her equality. Hierarchy of male over female is firmly ensconced by Yahweh's declarations.

We ponder Adam's need to be propped up by the drastic curtailing of Eve's natural being. The remedy seems extreme. Unlike An facing Inanna, Yahweh does not collapse before Eve's aggressive disobedient action. Like An, however, Yahweh is unable to tolerate woman's equality. He solves the problem, not by giving up as An does, but by diminishing the woman. His action is a curse women have borne for three thousand years. For men, on the other hand, diminishing women's power allows them to extricate themselves from the grip of the mother. The influence of Greek thought added the soaring of the masculine spirit away from the body, a split that dominated Greek philosophy and western thinking in general.

We live the consequences of our Greek heritage and of our envelopment in Judeo-Christian values. Diminishing the power of women and dismissing the connection to the natural world allows us to ignore the effects that the conquest of plant and animal life has had on the people of the earth. We are reaping the harvest of Yahweh's extreme solution.

Enheduanna intuited this impending split between body and spirit. In "Inanna and Ebih," Inanna destroys the sprouts germinating on the slopes of Mount Ebih. She casts the great god An in a humiliating posture. Inanna rises above him to dominate the sky as the star Venus and to dominate the earth as the one goddess who successfully passes into and emerges from the underworld.[32] Enheduanna establishes Inanna as the only deity who can consolidate the vast expanse of opposites in one being. She *is* primary, and whatever illusory power humanity may invent, she will reclaim with her irresistible, inundating flow. Gaining dominance in "Ebih" positions Inanna for the comprehensive visionary statement Enheduanna makes in the next poem, "Lady of Largest Heart."

▲ ▶

9

The Second Poem
Lady of
Largest Heart

Introduction

Of the three poems represented here, "Lady of Largest Heart" is the most complete statement of Enheduanna's theology.[1] Unlike the other two, this poem has no story line but appears to be a loose-knit collection of praise hymns to Inanna. Only at the end of the poem does Enheduanna tell us her purpose in writing it. She has undergone a long period of suffering, she says. Such suffering can only be caused by Inanna. She questions the goddess's motives. How can Inanna torture her this way when she is the most devoted of worshipers?

> I am yours
> why do you slay me

For Enheduanna's suffering to be lifted, Inanna must be soothed and calmed and restored to a favorable temper. Therefore, Enheduanna writes verse after verse praising Inanna's unequaled powers. The first long section of the poem is Enheduanna's attempt to get Inanna's attention and enlist her mercy.

In the process of declaring Inanna's superior might, Enheduanna tells us who Inanna is. This goddess has seized the world-ordering powers, the **me**, from the other gods and now surpasses them all, even great An. Not only that, Inanna is also the author of the "carved-out ground plan / of heaven and earth." She wears this plan on her royal robe. All gods, all creatures tremble before her.

By elevating Inanna above all other gods, Enheduanna has conceived, in 2300 B.C.E., the idea of a supreme deity. Granted, Inanna is not the only god or goddess in the pantheon. However, in Enheduanna's account, Inanna has gathered into her dominion powers greater than those of all the other gods. Moreover, only she possesses the ground plan of heaven and earth. Enheduanna approaches, in Jung's words, "a unitary vision of the world." [2] Enheduanna's Inanna includes the physical and the mystical. In Enheduanna's unitary vision, the god-image, namely Inanna, was the enlivening force in all matter as well as the mystical spirit that guided an individual's path toward the divine. Enheduanna's writing is the first record of these profound religious ideas.

Simon Parpola, in his study of the oracles of Assyrian prophets who lived a millennium and a half after Enheduanna's death, describes the central role of Ishtar in Assyrian religion, whose roots clearly reach back to the Sumerian Inanna. In Assyrian religion, Aššur is the universal god *and* the totality of the gods, says Parpola, "all the diverse deities being conceived of as powers, aspects, qualities, or attributes of Aššur." [3] This situation raises the question whether the religion is monotheistic or polytheistic. Parpola says, "The whole problem disappears as soon as it is realized that God can be at the same time both 'one' and 'many.' " [4] Ishtar is the oracular goddess whose words the prophets speak. At times Ishtar and Aššur are considered identical; at other times distinct. Enheduanna's elevation of Inanna to the supreme position in the pantheon is a precursor to the nascent monotheism that found expression in Assyrian religion. Like Inanna in this poem, the Assyrian Ishtar is the link between the divine world in heaven and the human world on earth. Inanna in "Lady of Largest Heart" has an intimate relationship with Enheduanna at the same time that she reigns supreme over all other gods in heaven. The separation between polytheism and monotheism begins to blur.

The poem "Lady of Largest Heart" divides into five sections. The first section is an invocation followed by a recitation of Inanna's fearsome powers. This section includes a grisly song of death. The second section of the poem describes a ritual called "the head-overturning." Inanna invented this ritual, the poet tells us. In this ceremony, an androgynous woman and man are consecrated as sacred attendants in Inanna's temple. Following their consecration, the attendants perform their special office as lamentation priestess and priest who sing to cool Inanna's troubled heart.

Section three of the poem is made up of a group of verses all ending with the phrase "are yours Inanna." Enheduanna enumerates the areas of human life Inanna owns or controls, an articulation of the **me** of the goddess. Many of these areas demonstrate that Inanna wields her power both in the outer world of human affairs and the inner workings of the individual psyche.

Following the "are yours" litany, Enheduanna continues to recite Inanna's powers. Finally, the high priestess speaks of her affliction. "I, I am Enheduanna" she reminds her goddess, and pleads with her to stop the torturous suffering she has inflicted on her. This closing section ends with a restatement of Enheduanna's unending devotion and a final hymn of praise.

"Lady of Largest Heart" encompasses the broad scope of Enheduanna's vision. Her theology is innovative and expansive. The play of her imagination is extraordinary. Her devotion to Inanna is unswerving. The poem allows us a rare glimpse inside the mind and soul of this brilliant woman who lived at the dawn of western civilization.

LADY OF LARGEST HEART

IN-NIN ŠA-GUR₄-RA [5]
by The High Priestess Enheduanna

Lady of largest heart
keen-for-battle queen
joy of the Annuna

eldest daughter of the Moon
in all lands supreme
tower among great rulers

queen of rare deeds
she gathers the **me**
from heaven and earth
surpassing great An

SHE of the gods has power
SHE executes their verdicts
before her matchless word
the great Anunna crawl
ever sneak away

An is ignorant of her plan
never stands against her command
she is changeable and hidden

SHE completes the great **me**
makes flawless the ordained powers
She foremost of the gods
pulls the nose-rope with her hands

she is a wood-clamp
pinching the gods
shimmering fear shrouds the mountain
strikes the roadways silent

she shrieks
and the gods start shaking
she raves

the Anunna quaver
crouch like a bending reed
at her roaring **dum-dam**
they grab arms and legs and hide
without Inanna
An is indecisive
Enlil cannot fix fates

who dares defy her
queen of lifted head
she is greater than the mountain

she speaks
cities tumble
  fall into ruined mounds
  their houses haunted
  their shrines barren

she shakes with rage
  demons throw rope snares
  bodies burn in blistering flare

the one who disobeys
she does chase, twist
afflict with jumbled eyes

fighting hand-to-hand
or hurling hurricane winds
she alone is awesome

fighting is her play
she never tires of it
she goes out running
strapping on her sandals

a whirlwind warrior
bound on a twister
she tears the king's robe
dust-dry south wind
sweeps at her bidding
leaves in its trail
breast-beating despair

lioness Inanna
crouched in a reed thicket
leaps to slash the fearless

mountain wildcat
prowling the roads
shows wet fangs
gnashes her teeth

wild bull Queen
mistress of brawn
boldly strong
no one dares turn away

greatest of the great rulers
a pit trap for the headstrong
a rope snare for the evil

where she spits venom
fighting erupts
tumult spreads the poison

her overturned fury
Holy Woman's rage
is a rampaging flood
hands cannot dam

a ditch of spilling water
she floods over a road
swamps the one she loathes

Mistress Eagle
her fiendish wings flap in foreign lands
those snatched
never are turned loose

Mistress Falcon
the wide stall of animals
she mauls
slashes the cows and bulls

woe the city under her frown
its fields lie barren

the Queen dances in its furrows
weeds spring from her footsteps

even if he wanted
An could not do a thing

Lady Brush Fire
burns the high steppe
Lady of Raging Battle
batters to submission

SHE
in the midst of havoc
shouting over the din
begins her sacred song
the song drawn with a stick[6]
carves her indelible scheme
she sings
>her bread is lamentation
>her milk is weeping
>bread and milk of death
>O Inanna
>bread and milk of death
>who eats it will not last

>who she feeds
>burns with pain of gall
>gags on dung

>her song sung
>with joy of heart
>in the plain
>with joy of heart
>she sings
>and soaks her mace
>in blood and gore
>smashes heads
>butchers prey
>with eater-ax and
>bloodied spear
>all day

these evil blades
the warrior flings
pours blood on offerings
so who she feeds
dines on death

this song she sings

in the wide steppe
the silent glare of noon
she turns to black
and shrouded light

she blurs the eyes
so friend's face
changes shape to foe[7]

she shouts from the faraway steppe
so fertile field
shifts to arid waste

her yowl
like Ishkur's[8] thunderclap
and windy howl
shakes bodies
makes all flesh quake

who dares oppose
her undisputed deadly fray
who dares behold
her savage fighting
weapon's play
that floods the earth with rage
washes everything away

Mistress Plow
the vacant wastelands
split beneath your tooth

before you
the high-flown proud
bend wily necks and
strain against your truth

works of her proud heart
the Queen alone creates them
most exalted of the assembly
she sits on the honored throne
spread out right and left

with a stretch of her defaming hand
she crushes the mountain to garbage
scattering the trash from dawn to dark
with mighty stones she pelts
and the mountain
like a clay pot
crumbles
with her might
she melts the mountain
into a vat of sheepfat

She is Inanna
Bearer of Happiness
whose strapping command
hip-dagger in hand
spreads radiance over the land

fish dragged from the deep
in her stretched-out net
never will slip through
birds trapped in her nimble cast
thrash in the fine-eyed mesh

what she has crushed to powder
never will rise up
the scent of fear stains her robe
she wears
the carved-out ground plan
of heaven and earth
who seeks her word
does not look to An
the great god assembly
prattles in confusion
cannot fathom her plan's execution

she holds the life of heaven
with her single hand

fierce Lady Wildcat
sovereign of the Annuna
Inanna
you draw men into unending strife
or crown with fame a favored person's life

* * *

Inanna
dressing a maiden
within the women's rooms
embraces with full heart
the young girl's handsome bearing[9]

the maid a woman evilly spurned
taunted to her face
sways beneath the wrath
thrown on her everywhere
her only path a wanderer
in dim and lonely streets
her only rest a narrow spot
in the jostling market place
where from a nearby window
a mother holds a child
and stares

this dreadful state
the Lady would undo
take this scourge
from her burdened flesh

over the maiden's head
she makes a sign of prayer
hands then folded at her nose
she declares her manly/woman

in sacred rite
she takes the broach
which pins a woman's robe

breaks the needle, silver thin
consecrates the maiden's heart as male
gives to her a mace
for this one dear to her
she shifts a god's curse
a blight reversed
out of nothing shapes
what has never been
her sharp wit
splits the door
where cleverness resides
and there reveals
what lives inside

the unafraid
who shun her outstretched net
will slip and snag in its fine-eyed mesh

a man
one who spurned her
she calls by name
makes him join
woman
breaks his mace
gives to him the broach
which pins a woman's robe

these two SHE changed
renamed
reed-marsh woman   reed-marsh man
ordained sacred attendants
of ecstasy and trance
the head-overturned **pili-pili**
the chief hero **kurgarra**
enter ecstatic trance [10]

they weep   they wail
they weary and wear out
singing songs to quell a god's rage

Mistress
all day   every day weeping
you no longer roam the heavens
crying does not sooth your heart
stop I say
enough
moaning unending lamenting
do not cool you down

Beloved Lady of Holy An
look at your tormenting emotions
all the time weeping
YOU mistress of the powers of heaven
YOU unequaled in the earth around you
YOU exalted all on your own
        heaven and earth cannot gird your fame
You match Enlil and An
        sit at the great right hand
You outshine in the cult shrines
You excel on your own path

grain shoots break ground in the furrows
young Ashnan   grain goddess
You raise on a sky throne
rains swell the thick clouds of Ishkur
he thunders out of the sky for You
when you stretched your hand
seized the great **me**
O Inanna
your victory was terrifying

the lofty Annuna
bend down
press noses in the dirt

you startle the sky
riding out on seven great lions

An fear-stricken
trembles before your dwelling
only when you sit

in his own domain
does his flesh not prickle

and he says

> the royal rites of kings
> the divine rites of gods
> I hand over to you

> all the great gods
> kiss the earth
> lie flat in the dirt
> the high mountain of carnelian rose
> the mountain of lapis blue
> did bend its nose to the ground

> only Mt. Ebih
> refused to bow
> held its nose high
> stilled the greeting hand
> in triumphant rage you tore Ebih
> ripped the mountain with smashing storm

Mistress
you outclass Enlil and An
your praiseworthy path shows forth
without YOU is no fate fixed
without YOU is no keen counsel arrived

* * *

to run   to steal away
to cool the heart   to soothe
are yours Inanna [11]

fitful wandering
speeding by
rising   falling
reaching the fore
are yours Inanna

to smooth the traveler's road
to clear a path for the weak
are yours Inanna

to straighten the footpath
to make firm the cleft place
are yours Inanna

to destroy   to build
to lift up   to put down
are yours Inanna

to turn man into woman
woman into man
are yours Inanna

allure   ardent desire
belongings   households
are yours Inanna

wealth   brisk trading
quick profits   hoard even more
are yours Inanna

prosperous business   abundance of money
indebtedness   ruinous loss
are yours Inanna

to teach   watch over
supervise   scrutinize
are yours Inanna

life vigor   fitting modesty [12]
male guardian spirits
female guardian spirits
disclosing sacred spots
are yours Inanna

to worship in lowly prostration
to worship in high heaven
are yours Inanna

the word of rejection
the word of riddance
are yours Inanna

(10 to 12 lines missing)

to hand out tender mercies
restore your heart to someone
are yours Inanna

heart trembling   weakness
shivering cramps   illness
are yours Inanna

to have a husband   to have a wife
to thrive in the goodness of love
are yours Inanna

to spark a quarrel
within love's lusty delight
is yours Inanna

to be negligent
tend carefully
are yours Inanna

to build a house
construct the women's rooms
furnish them
to kiss a baby's lips
are yours Inanna

to spread the leg stride
to footrace
to win
are yours Inanna

to mingle
the brute   the strong
the downtrodden   the weak
are yours Inanna

to intermix
high ground   low lying pools
peaks   rolling plains
are yours Inanna

to give the royal crown
the throne   the king's scepter
are yours Inanna

(13 lines missing)

to heap on lavish adornments
small   large   fine   wide
are yours Inanna

to grant cultic rites
guide their execution
are yours Inanna

to utter slander
words of deception
to speak unashamedly
even hostilely
are yours Inanna

to sneer at an answer
false or true
to say wicked words
are yours Inanna

to joke   inflame a quarrel
provoke laughter
to defile   to esteem
are yours Inanna

calamity   bitter woes
torment   wickedness
darkening the light
are yours Inanna

fear   panic   alarm
stifling terror
dreadful brilliance
are yours Inanna

triumph   hard pursuit
trembling sickness
wakeful quivers   sleeplessness
are yours Inanna

to muster troops
to strike   slaughter

raise the battle cry
are yours Inanna

brawling
blurring the eyes
clashing strife   murderous fights
are yours Inanna

to be all knowing
is yours Inanna

to build a bird's nest
safe in a sound branch
make indestructible
are yours Inanna

to lure snakes from the wasteland
terrorize the hateful
throw in chains   hold in bondage
are yours Inanna

to summon the hated
is yours Inanna

to cast lots
is yours Inanna

to gather the scattered
restore the living place
are yours Inanna

setting free
is yours Inanna [13]

* * *

merely open your mouth
and tables turn
your glance
clogs ears
never to hear
your frown blackens the light of noon
your heart picks the moment of ruin
the place you name trembles

what is yours
cannot be crushed

who dares oppose
your deeds
Queen of Heaven and Earth

no bribes sway
divine verdicts you say
Inanna
judge of the palace throng

more weighty than a mountain
is an oath sworn in your name
An cannot compete

when you heed your nimble wit
all the gods around
cast their joyless faces down
you alone are glorious
all gods
all heaven and earth
call you
Great Mother Cow

scarcely lift your eyes
the gods
openmouthed
attend

in your dwelling
the great gods stand
saying sweet prayers

and praise
your dreadful brilliance
gladly live
at your lofty breast

no sanctions cease unending praise
where is your single name
not glorious

(10 lines missing)

a sorrowful wail is your song
no one can overthrow your works
your rage tramples under foot

what your hand has made
cannot be shoved away
what you build by your design
An cannot dwindle

with An and Enlil
well-known in the assembly
O peerless woman
you have bestowed great gifts
with single tongue An and Enlil speak
and seize the people for your hands
the word you lay down
An shall not set aside
the "so be it" you say
great An shall not unsay
your "so be it"
is a final "so be it"
your "destroy"
is a "destroy"

what you proclaim in the assembly
An and Enlil cannot throw out
the oracles uttered on your tongue
never change in heaven or earth
a place you sanction
meets no ruin
a place you brand
does not last

your godliness
like Nanna-moon and Utu-sun
shines forth in the holy sky

your torch flames
heaven's four quarters
spreads splendid light in the dark

those warrior women
like a single thread
come forth from beyond the river
do common work
in devotion to you
whose hands sear them with purifying fire

your many devoted
who will be burnt
like sun-scorched firebricks
pass before your eyes

hands do not touch
your precious **me**
all the **me**
pass before you

you have realized
the Queen of Heaven and Earth
to the utmost
you hold everything
entirely in your hands

Mistress
you are splendid
no one can walk before you
you lie with great An
on an unblemished bed

what other goddess
can gather
the **me** of heaven and earth

you alone are sublime
praise your name

* * *

I
I am Enheduanna
High Priestess of Nanna
with single heart
I am devoted to Nanna

(20 lines missing)

I plead with you
I say STOP
the bitter hating heart and sorrow

my Lady
what day will you have mercy
how long will I cry a moaning prayer
I am yours
why do you slay me
may your heart be cooled toward me
I cry   I plead
for your attentive thoughts

may I stand before you
may your eyes shine upon me
take my measure

I
who spread over the land
the splendid brilliance
of your divinity
you allow my flesh
to know your scourging

my sorrow and bitter trial
strike my eye as treachery
tear me down from heaven
mercy   compassion   attention
returning your heart to someone
folded-hand prayer
are yours Inanna

your storm-shot torrents
drench the bare earth
moisten to life

moisture bearing light
floods the dark

O my Lady
my Queen

I unfold your splendor in all lands
I extol your glory

I will praise your course
your sweeping grandeur
forever

You
who can touch your divinity
who can match your rites

may great An
whom you love
beg your mercy

may all the great gods
soothe your temper
may you gladden
as you near
the clear blue lapis throne
of the Queen
may the high sitting-place
say to you
SIT

may your holy lying place
say to you
rest
give way
refresh

where dawn breaks
    Utu flares
may the people herald
your glorious divinity
O you who are Queen
may they declare your splendor

for you
An and Enlil
and all gods in accord
fix a great fate

to you
they give
Queenship of the Throne Room

and You
O Queen
say who of the godly sisters
is worthy of Queenship

Queen
Mistress
you are sublime
you are venerable

Inanna
you are sublime
you are venerable

my Lady
I have shown your grandeur resplendent
restore your heart to me

your great deeds are boundless
may I praise your eminence
O maiden Inanna
sweet is your praise

"Eldest Daughter of the Moon"

Lady of largest heart
keen-for-battle queen
joy of the Annuna

eldest daughter of the Moon
in all lands supreme
tower among great rulers

With these two verses Enheduanna begins her longest poem, "Lady of Largest Heart." As with all the poems, I worked with a specialist in the Sumerian language, Daniel Foxvog, while translating. We spent hours carefully reading each line. Coming upon troublesome words or phrases in the transliteration,[14] he would look at photographs of the original clay tablet or at someone's copy of the tablet's cuneiform script in order to improve the reading of the cuneiform signs.

The process of working on the poem with Foxvog took many weeks. Afterwards long sheets of yellow paper with the notes I had taken lay in a box waiting for me to begin the second stage of the work. In this stage I would read through the Sumerian, the possible translations and explications of the verses of the poem many times, trying to get a sense of the whole. Slowly, line-by-line, I formed what seemed an adequate, readable phrase.

Immersing myself in the whole poem, I found parts of it harsh and grating and wondered who the Inanna of this poem was. Would I be able to make sense of her cruelty, bloodthirstiness, and destructiveness? Here are some of the raw lines I faced:

giš-al-LUL sag mu-un-da-sìg-ge x giš-IGI.DÙ kú-kú/giš-[tuku]l-za-ḫa-da BAD im-x-x UR x [x] x[15]

"type of ax/the eater she smashes heads with it; type of spear, the eater; battle ax which does blood."[16] Sjöberg, line 46: "The . . . ax makes them tremble, the . . . ax, 'the eater', the battle-ax . . . blood(?) . . . ,"[17]

Or:

nisag-b[i-a] úš in-ga-an-dé-dé nam-úš-a sù-s[ù]

"into its/their first fruits/offerings she pours (also to dine, serve food) blood, to empty, serve up death, or make remote, distant, sprinkle" Sjöberg, line 48: "In their first offerings she pours blood, filling them with blood," [18]

Or:

(Text A) ^dinanna súr-dù^{mušen} [· · ·]. (D)[. . .]-e-ne tùr-dagal ^dinanna TAR-TAR. (Fa). [. . .] súr-dù^{mušen}-dinger-re-e-[ne . . .] (The texts, designated by letters [A], [D], etc., each contain exemplars of this line.)

"Inanna, falcon of the gods, tears to pieces/cuts up/the cutter of . . . or wide pen of Inanna/the cow pen/ravages the stall and bulls and cows." Sjöberg, line 32: "Inanna, the falcon among the gods, the wide stall she, Inanna, tears into pieces." [19]

Or:

lú-nì-kú[k]ú-da-ni zé mu-un-táb-táb-bé/in GAR KA-bi-a mu-un-x-x-x

"the person to whom she gives it to eat, she will cause the gall to heat up/burn — what is in the intestines/excrement possibly/contents of sheep's intestine — from that one's mouth." Sjöberg, line 42: "The one whom she gives to eat, the gall will cause him a burning pain, . . . in their mouth . . ." [20]

I had not encountered this Inanna in the story of Ebih. In that poem she had smashed the mountain and brought it down with a vengeance, but her wrath against the mountain could easily be interpreted as an assault in defense of her sovereignty. Here, in "Lady of Largest Heart," Inanna's bloody appetite and terrorizing revenge made me shudder. In verse after verse, Enheduanna spat out the punishment this vindictive goddess inflicted on her worshipers.

Finally, I began to see the poem in all its parts. I took the first line seriously. Hope in this poem hangs by a thread, and there in the first line the thread dangles: **in-nin sà-gur-ra**, "Lady of Largest Heart." Inanna who spins this chaotic and destructive world is "She of the Very Big Heart," the heart over-full, swollen, over-flowing with compassion and mercy. However, the hope her large heart engenders does not last. Within moments of relishing the vastness of Inanna's heart, the supplicant meets the goddess as cruel, violent, merciless, savage, defaming, raging, demonic.

The images in this poem shake and rattle a safe and predictable worldview. The images assault the psychological house that humans inhabit. Enheduanna turns normal patterns of thinking upside down and offers no secure shelter in their place. Either we are rendered groundless, or else we push this Inanna away, and distance ourselves with rationalizations: surely this vicious, violent goddess comes out of a remote time, no longer relevant.

After a difficult courtship, I have come to love this poem. In it Enheduanna articulates her profound version of the rock-bottom reality of life. In order to understand her vision, we must go back to the very beginning of time, to those human or pre-human ancestors who first began to tell each other stories in order to explain the mysteries of life and death, love and loss, creation and destruction in the world.

Enheduanna's vision appears to be in line with what we know of ancient religious expression. Archaeological evidence, deciphered by Alexander Marschack, substantiates, in rock and bone carvings made over thousands of years, that early communities in the Paleolithic oriented themselves around the phases of the moon.[21] After examining hundreds of carved bones, mammoth tusks, reindeer antlers, elephant tusks, Marschack confirmed his intuition that these were calendars noting the procession of the moon's phases over months, sometimes years of time. The moon's waxing and waning became the first predictable measure of time. The moon was not, however, merely a clock in the sky, but a living body intimately connected to the group of humans who watched it swell and diminish and disappear. It was a manifestation of the sacred in the sky, and, according to Marschack, the central symbol of a traditional story or myth around which the community organized itself.

The ancestral tradition of moon worship was Enheduanna's heritage. We know Enheduanna was High Priestess of the Moon God, Nanna, at Ur. Inanna, the poem says, is "eldest daughter of the Moon." While Inanna was the moon's daughter, she was manifest in the night sky as the planet Venus. Nevertheless, her powers span the paradoxical opposites often symbolized by the phases of the moon. The content of the poem which causes us to shudder can be traced back to the first moon watchers; for these early people saw the progress of the moon's phases, from dark to full to dark, as a paradigm of the cyclic processes they encountered throughout all life. Understanding the pulse of life's cycles to be the grounding principle of their religious belief, they placed vicissitude and paradox at the heart of deity. Their religion taught them to understand change as the inescapable intent of the goddesses and gods. Their religious task, then, was to expect dark as well as light and to contain that expectation within themselves.

The correspondence of women's menstrual cycles to the phases of the moon became the focal point of ancient religious ritual, expressing the containment of dark and light. British anthropologist Chris Knight presents a convincing case for the relationship of women's synchronized bleeding and the 'leap' to symbolic culture in the Paleolithic period. He states, "(Ovarian synchrony) provides the key to an understanding of symbolic culture—not in the abstract, but in the specific, puzzling ritual and other forms in which it first actually leaves its traces."[22] Speaking of Aboriginal cultures he says, "*The myths allege that ritual power originally belonged to women.*"[23] By means of rituals around menstruation these early peoples solved for themselves two problems that afflict all human beings, namely how to maintain one's equilibrium when threatened with destruction from the outside and how to stay balanced when confronted with disintegration of consciousness on the inside. Over these dreaded losses they had no control. However, once the losses were equated with the dark of the moon, they became predictable as cycles in the great turning of the cosmos. Consistently, they observed, the slim light of the moon's crescent would return. The grip the moon's phases have on human consciousness is clearly manifest in the Sumerian's ritual observances of the new moon, and the seventh and fifteenth days of the moon's cycle.

Menstrual seclusion rites reported by Judy Grahn in her book, *Blood, Bread, and Roses,* reenacted the time of darkness before creation, i.e. before the community had 'secured' consciousness of itself with its history and its created patterns of social and religious life.[24] The taboos against light, against touching water or earth, etc. that the initiates had to observe served to protect vital elements of community life from the psychological dangers represented by the darkness the young girls entered. The menstruating woman, particularly at menarche, was equated with the dark of the moon and the absence of precious light or consciousness. In the menstrual seclusion ritual, the women confirmed their ability to approach the dreaded state of darkness and chaos and still return to the light.[25] This ritual recapitulated the creation of the world, i.e. the creation of consciousness. Menstrual ritual taught generations of women to balance darkness and light and all their associated oppositions: life and death, creation and destruction, plenty and want.

Inanna is the goddess who embodied paradox at the heart of her nature. That the ancients understood the relationship between the paradoxical nature of the goddess and menstrual seclusion is illustrated in a hymn to Inanna. Here are the pertinent lines:

> Your frightful cry descending from the heavens
>   devours its victims
> Your quivering hand causes the midday heat
>   to hover over the sea
> Your nighttime stalking of the heavens
>   chills the land with its dark breeze.
> Holy Inanna, the riverbanks overflow with
>   the flood-waves of your heart . . .

> On the seventh day when the crescent moon
>   reaches its fullness
> You bathe and sprinkle your face with holy water
> You cover your body with the long woolen
>   garments of Queenship
> You fasten combat and battle to your side;
> You tie them into a girdle and let them rest.[26]

Inanna's menstrual bleeding, like that of the ancient women before her, is synchronized with the dark phase of the moon.[27] On the seventh day of the moon cycle, Inanna's menstrual period ended.[28] Diane Wolkstein says of this poem, "By joining the menstrual cycle to the moon's cycle in a monthly ritual, the wild, frightening, and disorderly parts of life are subsumed into a predictable and reassuring order."[29] At the end of the dark phase of the moon, Inanna's temper cooled, and she lets her ferocious rage subside and rest.

In the poem "Lady of Largest Heart," Inanna herself came to represent the world creating/world destroying force the ancient menstruating women had sought to contain. The historical shift from attempts to contain the powers of the unknown through menstrual ritual and taboo to vesting those powers in a single goddess represents a giant step in the evolution of consciousness. This transition took place gradually over thousands of years. That Enheduanna perceived Inanna in this way is clear in the poem "Lady of Largest Heart." Her characterization of Inanna as a goddess who embodied polar opposites is recapitulated in the Assyrian Ishtar who, Parpola says, "as the coincidence of opposites (is) the power of love joining the opposites, and governing them all." [30]

If Inanna encompasses the powers of heaven and earth, then she surpasses all other gods. This indeed is the message Enheduanna proclaims in the poem. In other Sumerian literature certain of the gods are said to be supreme; so in some respects, Enheduanna is following a familiar henotheistic convention. However, the extent to which she pursues her argument moves it beyond mere convention. For Enheduanna Inanna *is* supreme, and as high priestess she conveys this message to the entire populace through her poetry. Enheduanna positions Inanna as foremost of the gods. Her exaltation of Inanna is unequivocal:

> queen of rare deeds
> she gathers the **me**
> from heaven and earth
> surpassing great An

In many versions of a Sumerian myth that describe the distribution of the **me**, not only do the great gods create the **me**, but An decides the crucial question of who will receive each of these gifts of civilization. [31] Enheduanna turns all that around. In this poem, Inanna has appropriated an abundance of **me** surpassing great An himself. And further:

> SHE of the gods has power
> SHE executes their verdicts
> before her matchless word
> the Great Annuna crawl
> ever sneak away

What has brought about this radical and fateful shift? Enheduanna tells us it is fear. The gods are terrified of Inanna in all her guises.

> She foremost of the gods
> pulls the nose-rope with her hands
>
> she is a wood-clamp
> pinching the gods

shimmering fear shrouds the mountain
strikes the roadways silent

she shrieks
and the gods start shaking
she raves
the Annuna quaver
crouch like a bending reed

at her roaring dum-dam
they grab arms and legs and hide
without Inanna
An is indecisive
Enlil cannot fix fates

* * *

An fear-stricken
trembles before your dwelling

Only if we consider this poem in the larger context of what our fore-mothers experienced as their bodies swayed in synchrony with the moon, can we understand Enheduanna's insistence on Inanna as foremost of the gods. Of all the gods, Inanna alone has the ability to travel the precarious road between creation and dissolution. In an ancient Sumerian myth, "Inanna's Descent to the Underworld," Inanna alone dares the journey to the Great Below where she is stripped, beaten, hung on a peg to rot, and is brought back to life, transformed by her underworld experience. She braves the dangerous passage to the devastating edge of consciousness and returns to the upperworld empowered, wearing the very eye of death. Implicit in her care of Enheduanna is the binding love from Inanna's large heart that has the power to embrace and contain opposing forces. In her poem, Enheduanna establishes the primacy of this oscillation between the opposites.

Although this poem is from an ancient time, four thousand years ago, it is still resonant, striking familiar chords of feeling. The relevance for a modern woman or man might be partially obscured by the context of current culture, but the deep need to understand the painful paradox at the heart of matter, namely inevitable change and death is the same in any age.

"The Carved-Out Ground Plan of Heaven and Earth"

Throughout our lives we are confronted with what seems like a never-ending task: trying to grasp the full scope of reality. As children, we adapt to circumstances by using the psychological defenses available to us. As we mature, we have to confront the defensive illusions we have constructed. One by one, the illusions, particularly about our families, fall away. If our psyches can tolerate the loss, we continue to let in more and more of human nature's reality: its dark and shadowy aspects, its limitations, and finally, recognition of the fragility of our brief sojourn on this planet. Psychological maturity involves the ongoing process of integrating into our conscious, everyday selves the full range of elements that make up the psyche inside us as well as those elements that make up the world that surrounds us. Inevitably what we must face is a mixture of our motives and deeds, and the similar paradox in others.

This poem is about just such a confrontation. Unlike the gradual awakening that characterizes the process of confronting tragedy and evil for most individuals, this poem lays out a fully detailed account of horrendous events of violence, horror, and mayhem. Enheduanna's portrait of Inanna is of a goddess who includes every possibility imaginable. Inanna embodies the total pattern of events in the natural world, including the human psyche. She harbors the extremes, from the most horrible to the most beneficent. To see her is to see all prospects. Enheduanna presents the whole sweep of Inanna's plan before our eyes, and to know and to accept it is to live without illusion. The picture she draws is the very ground plan of heaven and earth:

> what she has crushed to powder
> never will rise up
> the scent of fear stains her robe
> she wears
> the carved-out ground plan
> of heaven and earth

This unpredictable goddess Inanna is full of contradictions. The **me's** she possesses, that is, her own elements of power, include kissing the baby's lips, restoring the living place, handing out tender mercies. Then, as though her benevolence were a sham, she embodies the most hideous destruction. She delights in carnage, head-bashing, body-burning. In-

22. *Winged goddess Inanna/Ishtar, her bird feet on two ibexes, illustrating her dual earthly and celestial nature. Old Babylonian Period, c. 2000* B.C.E. *Courtesy of the Louvre Museum,* © *photo R. M. N.—H. Lewandowski.*

stead of feeding her supplicants bread and milk, she fills their plates with blood and gore. She destroys cities, dries up fields, mauls animals.

> fighting is her play
> she never tires of it
> she goes out running
> strapping on her sandals

Enheduanna paints a complex picture of the goddess in this poem. With her vivid imagery, she will not allow us to escape or ignore Inanna's fiendish brutality. A goddess of order we can stomach, but a goddess who pours blood on offerings and feeds us bread and milk of death sends shudders up our spines. What force is this that batters and mauls yet at the same time holds society together?

The magnificent robe Inanna wears is embroidered with the carved-out ground plan of heaven and earth. Its folds are stained with the scent of fear. Inanna's propensity to crush to powder, to slash, to snare represents the ever-present terror of death and destruction, of fragmentation and madness that permeates every life situation. Most adults successfully repress these archaic fears, so vividly present in infancy and childhood. Archaic fear is present in humans' animal instincts for survival. We go about our ordinary lives only occasionally paralyzed by the hand of terror. Enheduanna releases images of hatred, brutality, and destruction from their repressed captivity. The scent of fear, she says, is an integral part of the divine plan. This plan, which Inanna wears, owns, and designed, lies just below civilization's thin veneer: the rules, the laws, the customs, the rituals by which we bind ourselves. The lives we lead from birth to death in our defined communities rest on the surface of ever-impending disaster. Inanna of course owns the rules, the plans, the laws, the customs, the rituals too, and she is ever ready to pull the plug, snatch the rug, lower the boom.

> her song sung
> with joy of heart
> in the plain
> with joy of heart
> she sings
> and soaks her mace
> in blood and gore
> smashes heads
> butchers prey
> with eater-ax [32] and
> bloodied spear
> all day

We humans have devised rituals for survival, for love, and for play. The thin wall of custom, however, does not exclude the view of the wildlands beyond. Probably we could not survive long in the presence of archaic fear, but even with our defenses, archaic fear seeps into our consciousness and into our dreams. Enheduanna's theology places senseless violence, random disaster, pain, fragmentation, and madness clearly inside the divine plan of heaven and earth. Any semblance of order humans may devise is no match for Inanna's destructive appetite. She carves her plan in the ground with a stick. Her scheme is an indelible piece of the very matter of earth itself.

Enheduanna's description of the divine in this poem is a relentless portrayal of ruthless power, anticipating some of the biblical prophets' hymns to Yahweh. In our modern world, tales of cosmic revenge are left to poets and dramatists. The language of mainstream psychology is squeezed dry of cosmic relevance and seems inadequate to translate Enheduanna's meaning. Yet the individual human psyche is the stage on which these dramas play.

Enheduanna draws a picture of a world without illusion. She emphasizes the horrendous, the aspects of life we tend to gloss over. Inanna's vista, she says, *is* the carved-out ground plan of heaven and earth, and the goddess is its keeper. As author of the plan, Inanna holds in her divine consciousness all that exists. Her being contains the totality of all things. With this portrait of Inanna, Enheduanna created the first written image we have depicting the unity of the created world or an absolute image of wholeness. Limited human beings confront Inanna at every turn. The votary is one who gradually takes in more and more of Inanna's reality. Enheduanna portrays the life of the devout in these two verses:

> those warrior women
> like a single thread
> come forth from beyond the river
> do common work
> in devotion to you
> whose hands sear them with purifying fire
>
> your many devoted
> who will be burnt
> like sun-scorched firebricks
> pass before your eyes

Against Inanna's divine plan, her devoted hone their lives. The life of the spirit involves a slow and painful awakening to Inanna's reality.

"Look at Your Tormenting Emotion"

If we look carefully for Enheduanna's motivation in writing this poem, we will find it near the end. Enheduanna is being tossed about, besieged by tormenting emotions that erupt as a direct result of her goddess's distress. Enheduanna is suffering terribly. Her own emotions assail her with sorrow and bitterness.

> I plead with you
> I say STOP
> the bitter hating heart and sorrow
> my Lady
> what day will you have mercy
> how long will I cry a moaning prayer
> I am yours
> why do you slay me
> I cry   I plead
> for your attentive thoughts

The poem is an offering to Inanna, a propitiation extended with the hope of cooling Inanna's rankled heart. For this reason, Enheduanna presents her goddess with a recitation that extols the full reach of her extraordinary powers. For this reason, she reminds Inanna she is superior to all gods.

The Mesopotamians felt themselves to be intimately connected to their gods. They believed that any prolonged human suffering was due to the overflow of a particular god's emotion. Enheduanna naturally attributes her torment to Inanna's out-of-control emotions. All the elements of the poem are directed toward cooling her mistress's heart.

> Mistress
> all day   every day weeping
> you no longer roam the heavens
> crying does not sooth your heart
> stop I say
> enough
> moaning unending lamenting
> do not cool you down
>
> Beloved Lady of Holy An
> look at your tormenting emotions
> all the time weeping

Inanna's distress swamps the atmosphere with volatile disturbance. Everyone, especially the High Priestess, is buffeted about in the wake of the afflicted goddess's condition. Enheduanna gathers all the elements of her creative abilities in this poem in order to persuade the goddess to relent. She reminds her of the **me's** she possesses:

> mercy   compassion   attention
> returning your heart to someone
> folded-hand prayer
> are yours Inanna

She calls the names of all the gods to help her convince Inanna:

> may great An
> whom you love
> beg your mercy
>
> may all the great gods
> soothe your temper

She lures the goddess with visions of peace and tranquility:

> may you gladden
> as you near
> the clear blue lapis throne
> of the Queen
> may the high sitting-place
> say to you
> SIT
>
> may your holy lying place
> say to you
> rest
> give way
> refresh

We can only imagine the scenario that produced this poem. Enheduanna was beset with a long torturous suffering. As a devotee of Inanna, she naturally attributed her suffering to the wildly fluctuating emotions of her goddess. When the goddess is upset, "all day, every day weeping," she inflicts her devoted with the fallout of her miserable state. Those who love her bear the burden of her torment. Their only recourse is to plead with Inanna to cool her heart. Enheduanna tries to change Inanna's mood by reciting this poem, enumerating Inanna's many powers.

The connection the Mesopotamians made between their own emotional suffering and the gods' is simply a variation of how we understand emotion today. An intense, sustained emotion is one of the signals that a deep, primary psychic pain from the past has been triggered. It comes unbidden, an autonomous force. Emotion is the trace of an activated archetypal pattern. Emotion is the repository of the archaic landscape within each individual. Emotion is the labile, volatile, energetic force linking chaos and order in the psyche. Riding on emotion, a person can go back in time and visit a primordial landscape, untouched by cultural influences. Transported by emotion we make all the stops along the full continuum of our psychological vista. At one end of the continuum we are beset by overwhelming primitive rage or terror or longing. At the other end, we experience a calm peace or the satisfaction of everyday accomplishment. The palpable difference in each of these locations is the quality of the emotion.

Inanna rides the waves of these archaic emotions. Enheduanna perceived Inanna as a vesicle of primitive emotions that could rupture in an individual without warning. It is Inanna who "blurs the eyes / so friend's face / changes shape to foe." It is she who afflicts the one who disobeys with "jumbled eyes." It is she who "floods the earth with rage / washes everything away." Inanna is the Holy Woman whose rage "is a rampaging flood / hands cannot dam." "Her fiendish wings flap in foreign lands." Scratch the veneer of civilization that adorns us, and underneath you will find prehistoric cauldrons of archaic, chaotic, primitive emotions.

Reading "Lady of Largest Heart," we begin to gain a sense of the woman Enheduanna. The boldness of her poetry and the magnitude of her understanding strongly suggest that she lived according to her own inner convictions, with freedom and courage. Clearly she endured the anguish of tormenting emotion, yet nonetheless remained true to her goddess. Enheduanna's long prayers to Inanna in this poem are not unlike a modern person's agonized confrontation with intense emotion. Secure in her faith that ultimately, the goddess held the carved-out plan for her spiritual passage through this time on earth, Enheduanna could endure the searing affliction of tormenting emotion. In the Assyrian cult of

Ishtar, the goddess enters the human realm and, like the Gnostic Sophia, is imprisoned in the body. The task of the devotee is to free this "holy spirit" from the body's appetites and limitations. Contact with the goddess can be made through the emotions; for, as Parpola says, Ishtar "occupies *the heart,* the center of the body universally regarded as the seat of emotions."[33]

Enheduanna describes a spiritual life that demands devotion. In this poem she offers us a portrait of four routes women may follow, four spiritual paths particularly suitable for women. The four are directions Inanna herself blesses and embodies: warrior, priestess, lover, androgyne.

Four Spiritual Paths

In the spiritual paths she describes, Enheduanna takes us far from the religious ideal of woman in Christian beliefs, Eve or the Virgin Mary. None of the four directions Enheduanna depicts—warrior, priestess, lover, androgyne—represent traditional female domesticity. The Sumerian pantheon did have mother goddesses, the most prominent of whom was Ninhursag, one of the traditional four great deities. Ninhursag was also known as Nintur, "Lady Birth Hut"; Aruru who had the capacity to start labor; Ninsigsig, "Lady of silence," who prevents harmful words from being spoken at the moment of birth; and Mudkeshda, "Blood stauncher," when she stops the bleeding after birth. Sumerian scholar Rivkah Harris says, Inanna does not reflect "the female domestic domain."[34] She is not the tamed wife and mother, heavy with child, her fury cooled and softened by impregnation, her protective instincts raised to shield a child.

Inanna is an unsubdued, multifaceted, energetic female force. She is raw energy bursting for expression. She is raw libidinous vitality. And she is the whetstone against which the devotee hones her course toward spiritual maturation.

Warrior

We meet Inanna as warrior in the first verse of this poem:

> Lady of largest heart
> keen-for-battle queen
> joy of the Annuna

Hardly have we begun to bask in Inanna's large heart when Enheduanna tells us she is a queen ever poised for battle. Once again we meet paradox as a characteristic of Inanna. She is both nurturer and warrior. She is goddess of the overflowing heart ready to pour her nourishment upon her votaries like the "Great Mother Cow" of a later verse, yet she is also the ever-ready warrior who delights in battle:

> fighting is her play
> she never tires of it
> she goes out running
> strapping on her sandals

In this guise Inanna has more on her mind than mere heinous destruction. Although sometimes bent on destruction, more often her warrior nature is tied to an exuberant zest, a joyful, voracious appetite for life.

> She is Inanna
> Bearer of Happiness
> whose strapping command
> hip-dagger in hand
> spreads radiance over the land

She carries her hip-dagger in a "nothing stands in my way" attitude. In this mode she does not hesitate to challenge any obstacle.

If this zest for life were Inanna's only mode of being a warrior, it would not be difficult for the modern woman to follow. Her hands-on-hips, legs-planted stand fits today's model of the assertive woman. Inanna's warrior, however, assumes much darker proportions further into the poem. She becomes the random destructiveness of natural disaster as well as the ravenous goddess of death. Enheduanna presents these two characteristics side by side:

> fighting hand to hand
> or hurling hurricane winds
> she alone is awesome
> Lady Brush Fire
> burns the high steppe
> Lady of Raging Battle
> batters to submission

Her deadly force spares no one:

> a whirlwind warrior
> bound on a twister
> she tears the king's robe

In this verse, Inanna is the capricious tornado striking king and commoner alike.

In the most grisly section of the poem, Inanna becomes a bloodthirsty maniac, a mad warrior:

> her song sung
> with joy of heart
> in the plain
> with joy of heart
> she sings
> and soaks her mace
> in blood and gore
> smashes heads
> butchers prey
> with eater-ax and
> bloodied spear
> all day
>
> these evil blades
> the warrior flings
> pours blood on offerings
> so who she feeds
> dines on death
> this song she sings

Inanna encompasses in her broad sweep the whole spectrum of the possibilities of "warrior." First, she epitomizes courage when facing the vicissitudes of life. Second, she embodies the fierce destruction within wild nature. Finally, she is the horror, cruelty, and bloodthirsty evil of war and violence.

With this image in mind, we meet with particular interest and amazement the devotees Enheduanna parades before us in her poem. As warrior, Inanna is archetypal, the internal pattern, the template which bends

and shapes the warrior in each individual. Enheduanna's warrior women
are a group of votaries striving to realize warriorhood under Inanna's
aegis. In a verse already discussed above, Enheduanna describes them:

> those warrior women
> like a single thread
> come forth from beyond the river
> do common work
> in devotion to you
> whose hands sear them with purifying fire
>
> your many devoted
> who will be burnt
> like sun-scorched fire bricks
> pass before your eyes

Images of a line of votaries threading their way to the temple at Ur
from a place "beyond the river" come to mind. Perhaps these warrior
women were an order of priestesses, a special group of women devoted
to Inanna, committed to surrendering themselves to her purifying fire.

Coming from "beyond the river" suggests that these women lived apart
from the population in a cloistered place. Beyond the river in Sumer
would have been near the steppe, or in the desert, both of which figure in
Sumerian mythology as uncivilized homes for demons, ghosts, and bar-
barians. In my metaphorical imagination, these warrior women lived in
close proximity to the wildlands of the unconscious. Like their ancestors
who entered the menstrual hut in order to meet chaos and disintegration,
and out of that meeting, recreate the ordered, conscious world, Enhe-
duanna's warrior women submit themselves to Inanna's burning fire in
order to emerge purified, the wildness and chaos contained.

The work of these women is common work. Their daily lives are ordi-
nary. Significantly, however, their work is entirely devoted to Inanna.
Each encounter with one of Inanna's gifts is a burning. The purifying
fire with which Inanna sears her many devoted is the fire of painful
self-recognition and sacrifice. Purifying fire burns away illusion. Sun-
scorched firebricks are cured and hardened and ready to support com-
plicated, sturdy structures.

Enheduanna is herself a warrior woman, in the sense that she lives her
life with great courage. Like the women she calls "warrior women" in

the poem, she accepts the searing events Inanna brings into her life, even enduring exile in the next poem, "The Exaltation of Inanna." With the bravery of a warrior she endures severe emotional distress, then writes of her experience for all the world to see. She even presumes to elevate her goddess above all other gods, a daring act that must have raised the ire of conventional believers. She probably guided the warrior women, Inanna's devoted, from across the river. As high priestess, she was probably spiritual director to these chosen women, teaching them the meaning of Inanna's searing fire. These two verses serve as a key that unlocks the meaning of the dreaded, fearsome Inanna of the poem.

Priestess

At the dim beginning of recorded history, only a thousand years after the appearance of the first examples of the pictographic script that later became cuneiform, Enheduanna, daughter of King Sargon, became the High Priestess of Sumer. While she lived in the south, in Ur, near the confluence of the Tigris and Euphrates rivers, her poetry reached the great temples throughout Mesopotamia. From her collection of forty-two hymns written for various temples, including temples in Eridu, Nippur, Ur, Uruk, Lagash, Sippar, and Agade, we find her traveling from city to city, praising the uniqueness and the local hegemony of each city's gods. Enheduanna's poetic genius, exhibited in the temple hymns and in the poems to Inanna, spread her vision and her influence to the populace of the entire kingdom.

Enheduanna effectively created the office of high priestess. For five hundred years after her death, a daughter of the ruling king became high priestess at Ur and followed Enheduanna's example. For Enheduanna, the role of high priestess meant living out the precepts implicit in the character of the goddess Inanna. So closely identified was Enheduanna with Inanna that as high priestess on earth, she saw herself as a mirror image of Inanna who was high priestess in the heavens. She says of Inanna:

> your hands seize the seven great powers
> rightly you are High Priestess.

Enheduanna's works are the first known written record of a religious belief system, elements of which later appeared in the cults of the Ca-

naanite Ashera, the Phrygian Cybele, the Egyptian Isis, and the Assyrian
Ishtar. In this work, Inanna is raised to the supreme position in the Sume-
rian pantheon. Her status is similar to that of the later Ishtar who is the
voice of the god Aššur, identical to him while at the same time being
a separate and independent deity that links the earth-bound material
world with the celestial. The concept of a female aspect of the godhead
carrying the whole spectrum of earthly life from the most heinous to
the most glorious is first articulated by Enheduanna. This concept re-
appeared in the Shekhinah of Judaism and the Gnostic Sophia, both of
whom could inhabit the confines of matter as well as unite, like Ishtar,
with the celestial emanation of the divinity. On earth, the complex She-
khinah represents the indwelling of the divine in humans just as Inanna
and the Assyrian Ishtar relate individually and personally to their devo-
tees, providing a bridge between the material world and the celestial.

Inanna in this poem "spans the tree of heaven / trunk to crown." Like-
wise the central symbol of the Assyrian Ishtar is the tree that Parpola
says "contained the secret key to the psychic structure of the perfect man
and thus to eternal life."[35] The tree appears in medieval Judaism as the
Tree of Life of Kabbalah, a primary symbol of Jewish mysticism. Ishtar's
cult was also a mystical cult whose devotees sought reunion with the
celestial deity through the burning and purifying stages represented in
the tree. This was the underlying process in Gnosticism where the fallen
Sophia had to be released from her bondage in matter through the purifi-
cation and sacrifice of the devoted, before attaining mystical union with
the deity. Enheduanna's poem introduces these and other concepts that
were later incorporated into other ancient Near Eastern religions.

In addition to suggesting a means of salvation for the individual, "Lady
of Largest Heart" also reveals the essential task of high priesshood,
namely to hold Inanna before the people as representing that paradoxical
nature upon which Mesopotamian beliefs rest. Enheduanna took upon
herself to worship, to contain, to appease, and to emulate this paradox
called Inanna by faithfully keeping the rituals of the gods.

The temple was the powerful center of Mesopotamian life. There,
within the temple, the forces of Inanna were drawn in, confronted, em-
braced, cajoled. Just as Inanna herself contained chaos and destruction
by enduring both and still surviving, so the high priestess contained
chaos and destruction within the temple by means of her ritual acts. The
task of the high priestess was to endure the inevitable hardships of her

historical era and to define and display for others how to worship the goddess whose plan determined their destiny. She pointed to Inanna as the explanation of the fate each person must live out. As high priestess, Enheduanna became the core of faith in a complex goddess who showered both blessing and curse. Inside the temple, chaos and disintegration were safely traversed through ritual enactment directed by the high priestess.

Inanna watches over and creates ritual for her worship. In her recitation of the **me**, Enheduanna says:

> to worship in lowly prostration
> to worship in high heaven
> are yours Inanna

As the ultimate high priestess, Inanna presides over worship from the lowest form of submission to the highest praise in the heavens. Worship belongs to Inanna. She is the source of ritual and symbolic definition.

> to grant cultic rites
> guide their execution
> are yours Inanna

Inanna has the power of inventing a ritual "out of nowhere" as the poem says. The earthly high priestess Enheduanna receives instructions on how to perform rituals from the clever mind of Inanna, the high priestess in heaven. Through the repetition and refinement of ritual, the worshipers confront the full face of reality as represented by the goddess Inanna and begin to assimilate the inescapable certainty of her rule.

Enheduanna lived during a time of religious transition. Many concepts expressed in her poetry evolved and were later incorporated into Near Eastern religions in slightly different form. Some elements were even incorporated into mystical Judaism and the beliefs of certain sects of Christianity. For example, the Kabbalah's Tree of Life, Parpola says, "can be shown to be based on a Mesopotamian model perfected in Assyria in the second millennium BC" (Parpola, XXIII). Likewise, the Assyrian Ishtar is "a divine power working in man" and must be understood "in terms of her human manifestation: she is the emotion moving the prophet, the breath issuing from his or her 'heart,' and the voice and words emerging

from his or her mouth" (Ibid., xxvi). In this respect Ishtar is compa-
rable to the Christian Holy Spirit or the Jewish Shekhinah, the indwell-
ing. We do not know the origin of these theological ideas, but aspects of
Inanna's image can be traced to Neolithic goddesses. A thread of beliefs
stretches from the sixth millennium b.c.e. to the present. In the context
of this continuum, Enheduanna is not only a brilliant poet and thinker,
but also a woman mystic inspired to write by her experience with the
divine Inanna.

Lover

Inanna is often described simply as a goddess of love, a Venus type. A
love goddess conjures up images of the seductive Aphrodite or Marilyn
Monroe. While Inanna can wrap herself in the allure of seduction, she
is a goddess of love in a much larger sense. She is that swelling of desire
which, as Diane Wolkstein says, "generates the energy of the universe."[36]
Inanna is strikingly similar to the Indian goddess, Kali. According to
Hindu belief, Kali is the primal creative principle underlying the cos-
mos. She is the energizing force of all divinity, of every being and every
thing. The image of Kali uniting with her god, she in the superior posi-
tion, is the image of this divine force bringing the universe into existence.
Goddess worship in the Indus Valley dates from 3000 b.c.e. Contact
between Sumer and the Indus Valley culture has been well established,
particularly in the Agade period. Gadd reports on finds in Mesopotamia
originating in the Indus Valley:

Especially clear is this in certain seals, found mostly on the sites of Ur and
Eshunna, which are engraved with pictures of animals belonging unmistakably
to the repertoire of the Indian seals, and the connexion is made certain by the
presence of the beautifully formed and still undeciphered writing of the Indus
people . . . Careful observation of the finds in Babylonia has placed most of them
in the Agade period, and although indications such as the etched cornelian beads
may suggest that the connection was older, it certainly flourished then as never
before or after.[37]

Unlike Kali, Inanna is not specifically portrayed as the generative force of
the universe. However, her arousal and sexuality is a blessing that engen-
ders growth and prosperity of every kind. In Mesopotamia the primary
focus of religion was to ensure the continuity of life through the fer-

tility of the fields, the animals, and the human beings who tended them. Sexuality became the principle metaphor for the continuity of life, and as such, it was a part of ritual in the temple, myths of the gods, and the daily life of the populace.

As a love goddess who foments sexual desire, Inanna's presence permeates every possible situation in which desire could be aroused. She does not differentiate between sexuality that is socially acceptable and that which is not, in contrast to the value system that dominates American culture. Inanna represents assertive, exaggerated sexual desire. In her listing of Inanna's me's in this poem, Enheduanna says, "allure ardent desire / are yours Inanna." Inanna exercises that power in the domestic scene, in the market place, in the temple, and in the brothel.

Inanna has the power to shower blessings of sexual desire within marriage.

> to have a husband   to have a wife
> to thrive in the goodness of love
> are yours Inanna

The verse following this one pertains to lovers in any situation:

> to spark a quarrel
> within love's lusty delight
> is yours Inanna

Inanna is watchful, ready to enter the space between potential or realized lovers and to fill that space with desire because all sexual arousal connects to primary being.

Sexuality, both in the temple of Inanna and in her ritual enactments and celebrations, is a more complex subject than the sexual arousal of desire between couples. First of all, the sacred marriage ritual, which may have culminated in sexual intercourse between the goddess and her consort through their earthly counterparts, is still a subject of controversy among specialists. Richard Henshaw reminds us,

there is no term for this practice qua institution in ancient Near Eastern texts. The term is borrowed from Greek literature, *hieros gamos,* and Greek ideas, especially Hellenistic ones, have been used in this study since its inception.[38]

Nevertheless, a body of literary texts, songs, and poems pertain to the observance of a ritual which a number of scholars refer to as the sacred marriage. This ritual enacted Inanna's role as the goddess whose desire engenders the life force itself. The union of Inanna with her consort fosters abundance and fertility throughout the land. It fills the "storehouse" with "cream and cheese and beer and oil" and showers a good fate on the individual worshipers.[39] By implication, this union, her arousal and desire, stimulates the energy of the life force in the land of Sumer and enlivens all beings to grow and prosper. Since the purpose of this sexual union is not pregnancy, Inanna's sexual enjoyment is the ultimate participation in, and affirmation of, the energy flowing through the universe.

The nature of the life force necessitates the enactment of the sacred marriage in order to link human life on earth with the revolving energies of the cosmos and the gods. For this reason Enheduanna reminds Inanna, "you lie with great An / on an unblemished bed." For life to prosper, Inanna must participate in the arousal of desire. Her union with An in the celestial realm provided a model for the earthly ritual. Sexual union as a metaphor for union with the divine recurs as an image in Gnosticism where Parpola says "mystical union with God, referred to allegorically as the 'bridal chamber,' constituted the highest sacrament in Gnosticism" and suggests that the " 'bridal chamber' is a blanket term for the whole gnostic initiation." [40]

Whether the so-called "sacred prostitution" was actually practiced is doubtful. However, as Will Roscoe says, the presumed practitioners are "referred to by modern scholars with that pernicious term 'temple prostitutes.' " [41] The suggestion of such an institution comes from Herodotus who reported: "the foulest Babylonian custom . . . which compels every woman of the land once in her life to sit in the temple of Aphrodite and have intercourse with some stranger. . . ." After presenting this passage from Herodotus, Henshaw asserts, "those of us who have studied Mesopotamian civilization for many years have never come across anything remotely near this practice." [42] Henshaw has gathered and organized the textual evidence of all the Near Eastern cultic personnel. Of the Akkadian *kezertu*, he says:

To translate simply as "prostitute" . . . indicating the street prostitute that word conjures up in our society is to oversimplify and neglect the cultic aspects, yet "odalisques of the royal harem" is too exotic, and to translate "sacred prostitute" is to go beyond the evidence, and to bring up all the problems associated with this so-called "institution."[43]

The texts suggest that there were temple personnel who, as Henshaw says, "symbolize, act out, pray for, rejoice in, and are part of the main purpose of the ancient cultus," that is the ongoing fertility of the country.[44] Some of the texts imply that the various personnel in specified offices engaged in sexual activity in the temple. However, the evidence does not document the activities of these offices.

Inanna herself enjoyed the life of the prostitute and was the protector of secular prostitutes. Inanna's ritual celebrations had a carnivalesque atmosphere where bawdy play and sexual license were the norm. Anne D. Kilmer reports one text that says that Inanna's "cult festivities" included "music/revelry, feasting, and fun in the house of joy and the tavern (the brothel)."[45] In "The Exaltation of Inanna," Enheduanna tempts her goddess by saying "I have readied your room in the tavern." Her purpose is to entice Inanna out of her bad temper by reminding her of the pleasure she enjoys when sexual desire is aroused. On the Early Dynastic Sumerian King List the queen Ku-Baba is called "tavern keeper," suggesting she presided over sexuality traditionally associated with the tavern.[46]

Inanna approaches sexual arousal with abandon, with revelry, with delight. She is a goddess of play, and her celebrations were noisy, costumed, song and dance, musical, carnivalesque affairs. She relishes teasing, caricature, flirtation, breaking the boundaries. She gets her way. To her consort Dumuzi she says:

> Dumuzi
> you belong in this house
> Dumuzi
> it is you I want
> for prince
>   and
> plow then
> man of my heart
> holy water-bathed loins

Source: tablet Ni 9602, column ii, obverse
   (my transl.)

The energy sexual arousal generates is the same energy that animates the warrior to take her courageous stance, the priestess to proclaim her adoration. Exuberant life energy flows in all directions. Sexual arousal imitates in the body of an individual the kindling of the life force. For Inanna this kindling of desire has a sacred dimension. Sexual arousal generates the arousal of energy in the plants of the field, the animals, the fertility of the earth. The sacred marriage ritual would have enacted this drama for all the world to see.

Androgyne

Inanna has appeared as Warrior, as High Priestess, as Lover. Now in a unique section of the poem, Inanna embraces and creates a specific ritual honoring the ceremonial aspect of persons of ambiguous gender identification.

> Inanna
> dressing a maiden
> within the women's rooms
> embraces with full heart
> the young girl's handsome bearing

Enheduanna describes the young girl using the Sumerian word, **la-la** which means "the vigor of a young man in his prime." The English word "handsome" best translates the cross-gender meaning, particularly as we read on and understand the context of the situation. The young woman in the poem, because of her manly appearance, bore the same ostracism in Sumer many androgynous individuals still endure.

Ceremonial androgyny has a long history. In Mesopotamia, the temple personnel involved in the worship of the goddess are often described in literary texts related to temple ritual as androgynous or sexually ambivalent, eunuchs, hermaphrodites, or transvestites. In modern times, some American Indian cultures make a place for the sacredness of cross-gender manifestation as in the *berdache* or the sacred dyke. Paula Gunn Allen speaks of the dyke in Indian culture as "one who bonds with women in order to further some spirit and supernatural directive." [47]

The gender-crossing priestess or priest has the ability to "cross over, to reveal two essentially different worlds to each other." [48] In that crossing, says Mircea Eliade, the original unity of world creation is revealed:

a coming out of one's self, a transcending of one's own historically controlled situation . . . a paradoxical situation impossible to maintain in profane time, in an historical epoch, but which is important to reconstitute periodically in order to restore, if only for a brief moment, the initial completeness, the intact source of holiness and power.[49]

The place of the so-called "third sex" in ritual has been observed for centuries. The Greco-Roman *galli* were called "a *tertlum sexus*—representatives of a third gender."[50] Will Roscoe suggests a number of explanations, including the transcendence Eliade describes. In addition he cites, "the violation of social boundaries, especially those as fundamental to daily life as male and female, tears the very fabric of reality for those who witness it."[51]

Cult personnel of ambiguous gender performed within the boundaries of the temple ritual. So contained, this tearing of the fabric of reality enables worshipers to contemplate the fragility of their constructed reality and to make a place for instability within their predominately stable world.

In "Lady of Largest Heart," the ritual consecration of the androgynous priestess and priest is similar to the "head-overturning" ceremony alluded to in "Inanna and Ebih." Later, in "Lady of Largest Heart," we learn that "to turn man into woman / woman into man / are yours Inanna." This piece of the **me** that Inanna commands has to do with cross-gender identification, with cross-gender dressing, and with Inanna's choice of temple personnel.

Inanna's cross-gender temple personnel appear in a number of texts. For example, in Anne D. Kilmer's rendition of a sacred marriage hymn to Inanna "the sag-ur-sag (cult entertainers) arrange their hair for the goddess; they decorate their necks with colored bands; they put aside their musical instruments and gird themselves with weapons for the cultic fighting; they wear costumes that are women's clothing on the right side and men's on the left."[52]

In the myth of "Inanna's Descent to the Underworld," the god of wisdom and of the sweet waters, Enki, creates from the dirt under his fingernails two "sexless" creatures to rescue Inanna, the **galaturra** and the **kurgarra**. Both the **galaturra** and the **kurgarra** figure as temple personnel in other texts, including "Lady of Largest Heart." In "Inanna and Ebih" we encountered the "head-overturning" ritual at the point that Inanna gathered temple personnel for her new temple. Now, in this poem, Inanna initiates a ritual "head-overturning" to "take this scourge," the derision heaped on this woman, "from her burdened flesh." She initiates a ritual to consecrate the sacred office this woman will enter.

Enheduanna brings us face to face with Inanna's androgyny. In the area of sexuality, as in all her character, Inanna will not be categorized. Rivkah Harris says, "She is neither here nor there. She is betwixt and between."[53] Inanna represents the full expression of the whole range of possibilities for woman's identity. That range includes same-sex unions. Inanna is free to travel throughout the landscape of her sexuality, enjoying each scene to the fullest. She sanctions sexuality in its many forms as the surging of the life force itself. To suppress a viable expression of sexuality, such as same-sex unions would be anti-life to Inanna and would go against the creative force of her nature.

The ritual aspects of androgyny connect to the sacred purpose of crossing over to reveal the other side, of belonging to more than one world. This spiritual crossing was more easily traversed by the androgynous temple personnel because they had already crossed the traditional boundaries of gender definition. In the instance this poem refers to, the newly consecrated priestess and priest must be able to go into ecstatic trance, to cross over from the conscious, everyday world into the trance world of spiritual ecstasy.

The **pili-pili** and the **kurgarra** of this poem belong, Henshaw says, to "a special class of officials, as a kind of actor in the cultic drama, whose forte is the interpretation of sexuality, but seemingly abnormal sexuality."[54] The etymology of the names is uncertain, though scholars suggest for "**pili-pili**" such meanings as distorted, disgraced, defiled. The **kurgarra** is a singer who also plays musical instruments and drums. He carries various weapons, chiefly knives, swords, or daggers. Sometimes these are covered with blood which one text says "delights the heart of Ištar."[55] D. O. Edzard, a noted and highly respected scholar of the Sumerian language, carries the notion of "dirty" a step further. He connects the etymology of these names to children's slang: the **kurgarra** (the **kur** being a mountain) signifying a small pile (of feces), the **pili-pili**, someone always making pee pee.[56] If he is correct, this etymology underscores the negative connotations associated with the temple personnel.

Inanna invents a sacred role for the **pili-pili**, the newly consecrated woman, and for the **kurgarra**, the newly consecrated man. She and her high priestess, Enheduanna, know well that the sacred defines forms of reality. To give non-specific gender a sacred place in the temple is to certify, to honor, and to give it a culturally substantial role.

Prior to the creation of the ritual for the **pili-pili**, the woman identified in Enheduanna's poem wandered as an outcast in the streets. Her street wandering suggests she was a prostitute. She was "evilly spurned / taunted to her face." She was outside the female domestic domain. A mother with her child stared at her from a window. This is the dreadful state Inanna would undo. With her advocacy of variance in gender identities, Inanna does not tolerate a biased and narrow view that privileges domestic heterosexuality. She validates the androgyne just as she does the priestess, the prostitute, the lover, the warrior. The manly woman wandered undefined by the sacred. She was living out a taboo of society and therefore was dangerous, a threat to the mother and child domestic scene. All this changed when Inanna gave gender ambiguity sacred definition.

Inanna invents ritual "out of nothing." In so doing, she connects ambiguous gender definition to a sacred archetype. The archetype in this instance is an innate ability to cross boundaries, to travel between the conscious and the unconscious worlds. Inanna declares ambiguous gender a gift of the gods and gives the newly initiated priestess and priest a specific purpose or office in the worship of the temple.

In her poem, Enheduanna makes clear that Inanna invented this ritual and established this priestly office because she wanted to "shift a god's curse" "for this one dear to her." "Out of nothing" Inanna shaped "what has never been." She opened the door of her own cleverness and created a brand new sacred office that would harbor the **pili-pili** and the **kurgarra**.

To perform the ritual, Inanna takes the maiden into the women's rooms of the temple, a specific place for women within the **gipar**. The ceremony to take place suggests that these rooms included a sacred space. These special rooms of the temple may have been the place where other rituals involving women took place. The women's rooms were a separate area in which women could be set apart and their spiritual needs attended to. It is here that Inanna begins the head-overturning by dressing this maiden so dear to her.

> in sacred rite
> she takes the brooch

> which pins a woman's robe
> breaks the needle, silver thin
> consecrates the maiden's heart as male
> gives to her a mace

Enheduanna describes the head-overturning of the man more briefly. He is "one who spurned her." She calls him by name, "makes him join / woman."

> breaks his mace
> gives to him the brooch
> which pins a woman's robe

His cross-dressing parallels that of the **pili-pili**. He takes on the traditional dress of a woman while she takes on the dress and emblems of power of a man.

Inanna renames these two "reed-marsh woman reed-marsh man." The reeds which were ubiquitous at the edge of the marsh by the rivers in Sumer define the space between solid ground and the sure flow of the river water. Inanna names her new priestess and priest after that strip of territory in between, the transition space from water to land, to identify them as persons who are able to live in the between-world space bordering the conscious and the unconscious. The **pili-pili** and the **kurgarra** are linked in other texts to the ecstatic.[57] Roscoe reports lamentations to calm the heart of the deity from the mid-third millennium that involved crying and wailing. He suggests this office might originally have been a female profession "later taken over by men."[58] In subsequent Neo-Assyrian time, prophecy and ecstasy were connected. Parpola recounts that "the 'possession' of the prophet by the Goddess involved a change in consciousness—purposely triggered by ascetic techniques such as weeping and wailing" producing oral prophecy as well as visions and dreams.[59]

Between her description of the maiden's rites and those of the man, Enheduanna places this verse:

> the unafraid
> who shun her outstretched net
> will slip and snag in its fine-eyed mesh

This warning, which Enheduanna repeats throughout the poem, reminds those who listen that Inanna's net enfolds all life. She pulls the strings of its webbing. It is she who has the power to turn man into woman, woman into man, who has the power to situate those dear to her firmly within her sacred domain, be they priestess, warrior, lover, androgyne. Should one blithely ignore her all-encompassing powers, that one will surely be snagged nonetheless, for Inanna throws the net around us all as a part of her immense design.

CHAPTER

10

⌄⌄

The Third Poem
The Exaltation
of Inanna

Introduction

After the diversity and fullness of expression of "Lady of Largest Heart," "The Exaltation of Inanna" stands in stark contrast. Despite the title, this poem is about an actual event that happened to Enheduanna. The part Enheduanna plays in each of the three poems I have translated varies. In "Inanna and Ebih," Enheduanna does not mention her own name, but we feel her presence as the singer of the verses.

> Maiden Inanna
> I worship you
> here is my song

At the end of "Ebih" she inscribes the poem with her characteristic phrase:

> Holy Inanna
> sweet is your praise

Then, at the end of "Ebih," Enheduanna identifies herself as a writer by paying homage to the divine force that guides her creations, Nisaba.

and praise be to Nisaba
goddess of writing

In "Lady of Largest Heart" Enheduanna introduces herself by name:

I
I am Enheduanna
High Priestess of Nanna

"Lady of Largest Heart" emanates from Enheduanna's emotional distress. As previously discussed, she wrote the poem as an offering to Inanna with the hope of cooling her goddess' heart in order to stem the tide of suffering Inanna's misery was spilling on the High Priestess. Enheduanna's presence permeates every line. She creates the imagery of "Lady of Largest Heart" and infuses herself into the poem.

Though Enheduanna figures in the first two poems, these poems are primarily about Inanna. The goddess is the leading actor. Enheduanna occupies a small but essential part of the text. With "The Exaltation of Inanna" we have an entirely different situation. This poem is about Enheduanna. She is the central character, not Inanna. The poem is about an actual event through which Enheduanna was exiled from her rightful place in the temple by a usurper, one Lugalanne.

Even with its favorable ending in which Enheduanna returns to her place as high priestess, "The Exaltation of Inanna" has an air of foreboding. In this poem Enheduanna faces a situation similar to that which Inanna faced in "Inanna and Ebih." Mount Ebih dared to defy the goddess and threatened to rob her of her powers over nature. In "The Exaltation of Inanna" a man overpowers Enheduanna and forces her out of the temple into exile, usurping her place. In "Inanna and Ebih" the battle is at the archetypal level of the gods. In this poem the battle is at the human level: high priestess against invader.

This poem appears to be the work of a more mature poet. All the elements of the other poems are here. Inanna is summoned in the first verses as the ultimate Queen. Her unquestioned dominion and her ruthless power are described in no uncertain terms. But there is a softness and a simplicity in these verses that is missing in the other poems. In "Ebih" and "Lady of Largest Heart," Enheduanna portrays Inanna's prowess in extreme terms. In "The Exaltation" she describes her goddess's superiority with a calm certainty. She does not find it necessary to convince Inanna over and over again of her bloodthirsty hunger. Enheduanna seems more sympathetic to Inanna's victims. Indeed, she becomes one of the victims herself.

The very personal nature of this story infuses the imagery with an added level of meaning because the sufferer is Enheduanna. For this reason, the "The Exaltation of Inanna" has a very different quality from the two preceding poems. It is the simple, anguished lament of a woman overpowered by brute force. Inanna's presence in the poem is still essential, but remains secondary to Enheduanna's suffering. The poem's theme of a woman's displacement, or fall, will have a familiar ring to modern women.

THE EXALTATION OF INANNA[1]

NIN-ME-ŠÁR-RA
by The Priestess Enheduanna

Queen of all given powers
unveiled clear light
unfailing woman wearing brilliance
cherished in heaven and earth[2]

chosen, sanctified in heaven
You
grand in your adornments
crowned with your beloved goodness
rightfully you are High Priestess

your hands seize the seven fixed powers
  my queen of fundamental forces
  guardian of essential cosmic sources

you lift up the elements
bind them to your hands
gather in powers
press them to your breast

vicious dragon you spew
  venom poisons the land
like the storm god you howl
  grain wilts on the ground

swollen flood rushing down the mountain
YOU ARE INANNA
SUPREME IN HEAVEN AND EARTH

mounted on a beast
You Lady ride out
shower the land with flames of fire
your fated word charged
with An's command

who can fathom your depths
you of the great rites

You
mountain smasher
give the storm wings

You
Enlil's dear
fling storms over the land
you stand at An's command
my Lady
the shriek of your voice
shatters foreign lands [3]

You
dreaded southwind
hurl a hot storm
people stumble   dazed and silent
face the terror of holy power
chanting a dirge
they meet you at the crossroads
of the house of sighs

at the front of battle
all is smashed before you
the obsidian blade ravages
my Lady
by your own arm's power

a gouging storm-bull, you gouge
a rumbling storm-roar, you thunder
you bellow with the storm god
you moan with evil winds
your feet never weary

you sing of sorrow
play the harp of lamentation

before you my Queen
the Annuna
all the great gods
fly away to the ruins
flutter around like bats

wither at your smoldering glance
cower beneath your scowl

your angry heart
who can soothe it
cooling your cruel heart is
too forbidding

the Queen alone lifts her feelings
the Queen alone gladdens her heart
She will not quiet her rage
O great daughter of Suen

Queen
greater than the mountain
who dares raise nose-pressed-to-the-ground
when the mountain quits nose-rubbing
you curse its grain
     spin ashes around its main gate
     pour blood into its rivers
     its people cannot drink
it hands over captives
armies disband
strong young men
come before you willingly

a wind storm breaks up dancing in the city
drives the prime youth before you
rope-tied captives

to the city which does not profess
"the land is yours"
which does not say
"it is your father's"
you speak one holy word
turn that city from your path

you abandon its sacred stall
the woman no longer speaks sweetly to her husband
     no longer tells secrets at midnight
     does not disclose
     the soft whispers in her heart

ecstatic wild cow[4]
eldest daughter of Suen
Queen greater than An
who dares withhold adulation

mistress of the scheme of order
great Queen of queens
babe of a holy womb
greater than the mother who bore you
You all knowing
You wise vision
Lady of all lands
life-giver for the many
faithful Goddess
worthy of powers
to sing your praise is exalted

You of the bountiful heart
You of the radiant heart
I will sing of your cosmic powers

* * *

truly for your gain
you drew me toward
my holy quarters
I
the High Priestess
I
Enheduanna

there I raised the ritual basket
there I sang the shout of joy

but *that man* cast me among the dead
I am not allowed in my rooms
gloom falls on the day
light turns leaden
shadows close in
dreaded southstorm cloaks the sun

he wipes his spit-soaked hand
on my honey sweet mouth
my beautiful image
fades under dust

what is happening to my fate
O Suen
what is this with Lugalanne

speak to An
he will free me
tell him "Now"
he will release me

the Woman will dash his fate
that Lugalanne
the mountains the biggest floods
lie at Her feet

the Woman is as great as he
she will break the city from him
        (may her heart grow soft for me)

stand there
I
Enheduanna   Jewel of An
let me say a prayer to you
        (flow tears
        refreshing drink for Inanna)

I say to Her
silim [5]
be well

I say
I no longer soothe Ashimbabbar

all the cleansing rites of Holy An
that man changed them

he robbed An of his temple
        he does not fear Big Man An
the potent vigor of the place

does not fill him
he spoiled its allure
truly he destroyed it

haunt him
with the ghost
of her you set up as your partner

O my divine ecstatic wild cow
drive this man out
hunt him down
catch him

I
who am I
in the place which holds up
life's key elements

may An desert those rebels
who hate your Nanna
may An wreck that city
may Enlil curse its fate
may the mother not comfort
her crying child

Queen
creator of heart-soothing
that man junked
your boat of lamentation
on an alien sea

I am dying
that I must sing
this sacred song
I
even I
Nanna ignores my straits
am I to be ruined by treachery
I
even I
Ashimbabbar
neglects my case

whether he neglects me
or not
what does it matter
that man threw me out of the temple
I who served triumphant

he made me fly
like swallows swept
from their holes in the wall

he eats away at my life
I wander through thorny brush in the mountains
he robbed me
of the true crown
of the High Priestess

he gave me
the ritual dagger of mutilation
he said
"it becomes you"

precious Queen
loved by An
rekindle for me
your holy heart

beloved wife of the sky dragon
        Ushumgalanna [6]
Great Lady
who spans the tree of heaven
trunk to crown
all the Annuna
lash yoke over neck for you

You
born a minor queen [7]
how great you have become
greater than the Anunna
greater than the Great Gods

the Anunna
press lips to the ground for you

that man has not settled my claim
again and again
he throws a hateful verdict
in my face

I no longer lift my hands
from the pure sacred bed
I no longer unravel
Ningal's gifts of dreams
to anyone

I
most radiant priestess of Nanna
may you cool your heart for me
my Queen
beloved of An

PROCLAIM!
PROCLAIM!
I shall not
pay tribute to Nanna
it is of YOU
I PROCLAIM

that you are exalted as An
PROCLAIM!

that you are wide as earth
PROCLAIM!

that you crush rebellious lands
PROCLAIM!

that you shriek over the land
PROCLAIM!

that you smash heads
PROCLAIM!

that you gorge on corpses like a dog
PROCLAIM!

that your glance flames with rage
PROCLAIM!

that you throw your glance around
PROCLAIM!

that your eyes flash like jewels
PROCLAIM!

that you balk and defy
PROCLAIM!

that you stand victorious
PROCLAIM!

I have not said this of Nanna
I have said it of YOU
my phrases glorify YOU
    who alone are exalted
my Queen
beloved of An

I have spoken
of your tempestuous fury

* * *

I have heaped up coals in the brazier
I have washed in the sacred basin
I have readied your room
    in the tavern [8]
(may your heart be cooled for me)
suffering bitter pangs
I gave birth to this exaltation
for you my Queen

what I told you in the dark of night
may the singer recount at noon

child of yours   I am a captive
bride of yours   I am a captive [9]
it is for my sake your anger fumes
your heart finds no relief

* * *

the eminent Queen
guardian of the throne room
receives her prayer

the holy heart
of Inanna
returns to her

the day is favorable
she dresses lavishly
in woman's allure

she glows with beauty's shine
like the light of the rising moon
Nanna lifts her
into seemly view

at the sound of Ningal's prayer
the gate posts open
    Hail
    Be Well

* * *

this poem
spoken for the sacred Woman
is exalted
praise the mountain destroyer
praise Her who
    (together with An)
received the unchanging powers
praise my lady wrapped in beauty
PRAISE BE TO INANNA

"He Robbed Me of the True Crown"

Enheduanna has been removed from her office of high priestess by force. Banished from Nanna's temple at Ur. The story she tells appears actually to have happened.[10] A man named Lugalanne or Lugalanna, according to Hallo and van Dijk, "played a role in the great revolt against Naram-Sin" at Uruk. They find no reason to believe this was not the same person in the poem.[11] Enheduanna's appointment by Sargon was an affront to the local priests; perhaps her expulsion was the result, as Nissen contends.[12]

She is wretched, alone. A wanderer in the wild mountains. Her clothing torn. Her face covered with dust. "He eats away at my life," she says. Her rage and anguish grow like a fetus forming in the damp inner chamber. Enheduanna swells with outrage at what has happened to her. She cries out to Inanna, and, in the bitter pangs of a figurative pregnancy forced upon her, she gives birth to a poem. She prays in the dark of night to her Goddess, anguish mimes the forced stretching to the edge of endurance, the tearing pain of birth.

> suffering bitter pangs
> I gave birth to this exaltation
> for you my Queen

Enheduanna uses the metaphor of birth to describe the process of "conceiving the word," a convention found in other Sumerian texts, for example the later King Gudea who "conceived or received the notion of building the temple of Ningirsu" in a dream.[13] These verses contain a unique description of the creative process of the poet, unparalleled in Mesopotamian literature. Enheduanna says she spoke to her goddess in the night, a familiar time of creative inspiration. She may have had a relevant dream. She was certainly qualified to be her own dream interpreter, as Hallo and van Dijk attest.[14]

The poem must match exactly the cosmic situation, must include all the elements. Then like a poultice it will draw out the poison and heal the wound. Enheduanna will return to her rightful place in harmony with the natural order that Lugalanne has upset.

Lugalanne's daring overthrow of Enheduanna is an ominous sign of things to come. The usurper is cruel. He has entered her rooms. He

mocks the dearest source of her being: her poetry. He spits in his hand
and smears her mouth. He defiles the sweet, honeyed tongue. He jabs at
her with the sacred dagger of mutilation. He says, "It becomes you." He
seems to be saying, "Use it on yourself!" "You know how the eunuchs
do it. Cut out your own sex!" He would have her sexless. He would pull
her from the pure, holy bed of the sacred marriage, ban her from that
ritual axis around which the year turns. He casts her out. He has effec-
tively undone all that Enheduanna created. He may even have assaulted
her sexually.[15]

First he silences her voice:

> he wipes his spit-soaked hand
> on my honey sweet mouth

Enheduanna's most effective means of teaching was her poetry and reli-
gious song. He spits on it. His hatred of her honey sweet mouth muffles
the outpouring of her creative genius. Not only that, but he tramples
her beautiful image under dust. Enheduanna, who created the role of
high priestess as poet—a model followed for five hundred years after her
death—is defiled by the brute force of a usurping man.

He invites her to mutilate herself with the ritual dagger "in the manner
of the androgynous dervishes (**kur-gar-ra**)" adding "insult to injury," as
Hallo and van Dijk observe.[16] The ritual knives of the temple belong to
the priestly attendant, the **kurgarra**. Self-mutilation, Parpola says, "was
widely practiced not only in Mesopotamia but all over the ancient Near
East, and illustrates the tremendous power that the cult of Ištar (Inanna)
exerted upon its initiates."[17] Lugalanne asks Enheduanna to bloody her-
self in vicious ways not related to the sacred blood of menstruation. He
wants her sexless. He wants her blood desecrated. He taunts and teases
and cajoles her to turn the ritual knife on herself.

He spits on her poetry. He befouls the ritual dagger. Then:

> again and again
> he throws a hateful verdict
> in my face

Enheduanna is reduced to begging this treacherous man for justice. He
responds with hateful, vindictive judgments against her.

Ultimately he drives her from the temple. She is no longer allowed in her rooms, her intimate space in the **gipar**. She is cast among the dead in the marginal wasteland of graves and tombs. He whisks her away:

> like swallows swept
> from their holes in the wall

She wanders alone in the "thorny brush of the mountains." She has lost everything, her triumphant stature as High Priestess, her true crown. She cries out in utter hopelessness and despair. In the wrenching pangs of hard labor, she gives birth to this entreaty to Inanna. Inanna is her only hope for rescue.

Armed men probably accompanied Lugalanne in his overthrow of Enheduanna. Such men were not new to her. Enheduanna had watched her father, brothers, and nephew send armies to foreign lands and return victorious. Lugalanne was apparently an enemy of Naram-Sin's, trying to gain prominence in the southern provinces of Sumer. Ur and Uruk had traditionally formed an alliance, and Lugalanne of Uruk attempted to free the provinces from the central rule of the Sargon dynasty. Enheduanna, who may have served the temple in Uruk as well as Ur, would have lost her position in both cities. The dreadful consequence of Lugalanne's action was the desecration of the sacred precincts of the temples of An and Inanna in Uruk as well as Nanna in Ur. He defiled An:

> he robbed An of his temple
> he does not fear Big Man An
> the potent vigor of the place
> does not fill him
> he spoiled its allure
> truly he destroyed it

Lugalanne enacts a masculine power beyond even that of great An.

If we remember Ebih, we know An's potency collapsed before the radiance of the mountain. Enheduanna makes clear in "Ebih" and in "Lady of Largest Heart" that Inanna's power is greater than An's. In spite of the domination of men in the political and economic sphere at this time, the male gods' superiority was equivocal, clearly present in some myths and missing in others. In this poem An again collapses in the face of a more powerful masculine presence, Lugalanne. Once again the secular overcomes the sacred.

A few figures of male gods have been found in Mesopotamia from the Neolithic period; but during this time, all divinities continued to exist as a part of nature's great design. Ultimately nature belonged to the goddesses, to the archetypal feminine, and to the teachings and ritual enactment of the women in the temple.

In Enheduanna's thinking, An, too, existed within this paradigm. His masculinity, as Enheduanna points out over and over again, is subject to Inanna's superior command. As we learned in "Ebih," to overthrow the goddess is unthinkable. All creatures, on earth and in the heavens, are subject to nature's ebb and flow, to the constrictions of the laws of matter. To defy this fundamental reality, the carved-out ground plan that Inanna wears on her robes, is an act of appalling pride and insolence. Inanna will unleash all her forces in order to crush such an audacious rebellion.

The goddess rules the masculinity of the gods, even An's. Among the priests, phallic masculinity is tempered, sometimes by emasculation, sometimes by androgynous dress and behavior. Theirs is the ultimate act of defiance against the domination of the phallus, facilitating, as Roscoe says, "escape from irreconcilable tensions by rendering oneself incapable of fulfilling either the social or sexual demands of patriarchal male roles." [18] Parpola maintains that the purpose of these emasculating acts "was to turn the devotee into a living image of Ištar: an *androgynous* person totally beyond the passions of the flesh." [19] Lugalanne enacts another sort of masculinity altogether. His attitude toward An's temple is this:

> the potent vigor of the place
> does not fill him

Lugalanne is no longer satisfied by An's potency in relation to the goddess. He brings an entirely new phallic power into the sacred precinct. Lugalanne attempts to carry out what Ebih dared to dream: the overthrow of the goddess. His bearing is that of a man no longer dominated by women or the forces of the archetypal feminine. Not only do his acts privilege the secular over the sacred, but his defiance of the goddess paves the way for the new masculinity of the ensuing monotheism of Judaism and Greek influenced Christianity.

The surge of phallic power that fueled Lugalanne's revolt, Sargon's conquests, and even the rise of kings in the five hundred years prior to Sargon's rule represented a new force not apparent in the Neolithic cultures dominated by the nature-centered religions. This torrent of male libido ultimately could not be contained or controlled by religious taboo.

Men tended to express this new freedom in two ways: through domination and creativity. Male dominance greatly increased as a result of the new weaponry made possible by the invention of bronze. This invention ushered in a new kind of military conquest. As they gained military power, men increasingly dominated the political sphere, economics, and social life. While Sargon was a life-long devotee of Ishtar/Inanna, the city goddess of Agade, his grandson Naram-Sin declared himself a god and on his **stele** of conquest, Figure 19, wears the singular horned crown reserved for a deity.

As male dominion of cultural life increased, the new freedom men enjoyed gave rise to a creative soaring of the imagination above the material plane. In classical Greece, the male mind reigned supreme, and with respect to the Romans, Marie Louise von Franz says, "The phallus symbolized a man's secret genius, the source of his physical and mental creative power, the dispenser of all his inspired or brilliant ideas and of his buoyant joy in life."[20] Men have dominated the creative life of the mind in the centuries since the beginning of monotheism. Whatever factors brought this about, men's exercise of their physical strength and appropriation of their creative freedom, part and parcel of a male-dominated culture, heralded an entirely new alignment of civilization, one in which their genius soared while women lost ground. By the seventh century B.C.E., all images of the goddess which had remained in the Hebrew temples were destroyed.[21]

In the process of monotheism's development, women suffered a great loss. The essential role women had played in ancient religions as guardians who contained opposites diminished. Women's roles became marginalized and secondary to the roles of men not only in the religious sphere, but also in the realms of politics, economics, social, and cultural life.

Men are captive to the patriarchal ethos and suffer stifling limitations as a result. In his interpretation of the myth of Attis, the castrated son in the Cybele and Attis myth, Roscoe describes the modern plight of many men:

Attis is the object of unwanted heterosexual overtures, caught between the social demands of the pater-familias and the emotional demands of a mother figure who is herself caught up in the dynamics of patrilineal sexuality and marriage. . . . [I]n polytheism gender ambiguity is given a different valuation, and sexual tensions can be freely projected onto female deities. It is the combination of these two factors—patrilineal social order and polytheistic religion—that creates the ground for the long-term appeal of goddess figures and their priests . . . The underlying hostility of this act (self-castration) underscores the transgressive nature of being nonmasculine and nonreproductive in a patriarchal culture.[22]

We who come of age within the basic assumptions of monotheism rarely think about how this paradigm infiltrates every corner of our psychological lives. It does not occur to us that our most entrenched values of good and evil, perfection and impurity, worthiness and corruption are strongly influenced by the splitting which male monotheism imposes on our socialization from birth. It takes a concentrated awareness to realize that this paradigm excludes all other possibilities, and to conceive that our most fundamental presumptions could be different.

"Rekindle Your Holy Heart"

At the beginning of this new millennium, no sacred place exists where we can learn from deep traditional lore what it means to be a woman. The evolution of consciousness has tossed us into a cultural maze where society assigns the highest values to the activities that take place in shopping malls or high-rise office buildings. In this confusing time women have only themselves to rely on. Connection to the sacred female seems to be possible solely in the resonant halls of a seeker's inner, imaginal chambers. The guide who will take our hands must be one of our own discovery. We look to myth, to ancient tradition, to writers like Enheduanna to show us the way. Each woman is on her own.[23]

Enheduanna offers a fitting model. Although she came to power within a centuries-old religious tradition that held women in high regard, she engaged in a private inner dialogue with her goddess, Inanna. Her life of attentive devotion to the inclusive female divinity, envisioned as the spark of being in matter, provides a model to follow.

In the temple Enheduanna performed the public rites to Nanna and to Ningal:

> there I raised the ritual basket
> there I sang the shout of joy[24]

In the inner rooms of her soul, she offered her solitary devotion to Inanna. In this poem Enheduanna provides an intimate glimpse of her private relationship to Inanna.

Exiled in the wild mountains, Enheduanna turns to Inanna for solace. Through the dust and gloom the dreaded southstorm showers on Enheduanna shines a beam of light. In her anguish, hopelessness, and despair, she still declares her ardent love for Inanna. Inanna chose her in the beginning, singled her out, and drew her to her office of the high priestess:

> truly for your gain
> you drew me toward
> my holy quarters
>
> I
> the High Priestess
> I
> Enheduanna

Theirs is a bond of mutuality. Inanna is high priestess in heaven. Enheduanna is high priestess on earth. According to Hallo and van Dijk, the poem recounts "the fate of Enheduanna, paralleling that of Inanna, in almost autobiographical terms." Parallels in the later "Inanna laments," recount "that deity's exile from her temples . . . described in a manner wholly reminiscent of Enheduanna's removal from the priesthood" in this poem.[25] The mystical parallels between Enheduanna and Inanna exemplified the interaction of gods and humans in Mesopotamia. Parpola attests:

It is thus clear that the distribution of the roles of the goddesses was not fortuitous but had a well-established doctrinal basis shared by contemporary prophecy, mysticism and royal ideology . . . the complementarity of the celestial and mundane realms, the latter being conceived of as the mirror image of the former.[26]

Enheduanna found her life's meaning in relationship to Inanna. Inanna called her from the traditional way of being a woman in her society, and summoned her to a life of religious devotion to one goddess, herself. That transformation occurred in the inner recesses of Enheduanna's soul. Her relationship to Inanna is that of her ego consciousness to a spontaneous movement in her inner world, the surge of emotion and image that arise as she conjures up the presence of Inanna. She experiences being Inanna's child. In Assyrian times, royal children were nurtured in the temples of Ishtar, "almost certainly to be suckled and nursed by hierodules who impersonated the motherly aspects of the goddess," says Parpola.[27] A prophecy of Ishtar to the crown prince Assurbanipal says:

> I will carry you on my hip like a nurse, I will put you between my breasts (like) a pomegranate. At night I will stay awake and guard you; in the daytime I will give you milk. . . .[28]

Enheduanna's experience of the nourishing Inanna/Ishtar may represent an early instance of this long tradition.

Enheduanna also called herself bride of Inanna. For Enheduanna love was aimed at a specific image, Inanna. Inanna became the organizing framework in her imagination, a real presence in the psyche with a particular character and a particular set of emotions. The image Enheduanna had of Inanna was, of course, influenced by the society she lived in, but the interplay of image and emotion in her inner world was a spontaneous motion, an autonomous dynamic over which the ego had no control. Her relationship to Inanna was utterly personal and unique.

As mentioned at the outset, for Enheduanna, Inanna was a personification of the ordered totality of "What Is." Inanna was a constellation of a larger, yet personally related, reality to which Enheduanna had access in thought and in imagination. As an image, Inanna shaped Enheduanna's sense of her own true nature, her essence, and meaningful purpose. The goddess, as a divine image of the Real, reflects the numinous order of the whole, against which the worshipful high priestess defines in her small, human way her own vocation. As high priestess, she becomes the conduit that expresses the essence of the Real to worshipers on earth. Enheduanna's relationship to Inanna developed into one of love for the divine.

Inanna lives on two planes. She is a goddess, a vessel of the divine, and she is a part of Enheduanna's intimate life. She lives both in the realm of the gods and in the realm of the individual soul. She spans the bridge between the celestial and the human. This paradigm continued in the

Assyrian Ishtar, the Hebrew Shekhinah, and the Gnostic Sophia, all of whom connect the divine to the earthly and human worlds. The Catholic doctrine of the assumption of the Virgin and the Christian Holy Spirit are vestiges of this tradition as well.

In the invocation of this poem, Enheduanna makes it clear that Inanna is an exceptionally powerful goddess. She is "Queen of all given powers" and "unveiled clear light." She is "chosen, sanctified in heaven" and "Queen of fundamental forces/guardian of unchanging cosmic sources." As mistress of the given forms and powers in the cosmos, she sways in a cosmic dance with her forces:

> you lift up the elements
> bind them to your hands
> gather in powers
> press them to your breast

The invocation of this poem, as in the other two, serves to locate Inanna, "supreme in heaven and earth," as the instigator and the life force who rides the unleashed energies of storm, wind, flood, fire, and battle. Inanna has the will and the force to curse grain, pour blood in rivers, abandon stalls, and drive people to the edge of unbearable sorrow.

Enheduanna states unequivocally that Inanna is much larger than human will, a terror even to the gods. She is a personification of the mystery of the forces of the universe. She is not merely Enheduanna's ego-ideal. Inanna is not Enheduanna's self-image. She is a force of the divine mystery of the cosmos, a goddess with particular attributes, characteristics, and powers.

The appearance of Inanna in Enheduanna's psyche was the beginning of a life-long relationship. While Enheduanna never doubted Inanna's divine force, she dared to relate to Inanna personally. Inanna became an intimate companion and guide, while maintaining her totally unique status among the gods.

PROCLAIM!

In the past thirty years women have imagined a religion centered on goddess worship and have begun to reconstruct the myriad pieces of an actual ancient religion whose core was female.[29] Now we have a written articulation of one woman whose religious tradition reaches back to the Neolithic age.

In the cultures of the western world, dominant religions have perpetuated a silence that has surrounded us for four thousand years. Now Enheduanna's voice has broken that protracted silence. Archaeologists have unearthed thousands of images of goddesses from Paleolithic, Neolithic, and Bronze Age. Building on these findings, women are beginning to piece together a cultural past in which their place in society was vastly different than it is now. In ancient times, women's social status derived from a religion in which femaleness was distinctly defined and worshiped and in which their role was central.

Enheduanna's writing is a poetic description of the full range of femaleness. Her work has archetypal dimension, and therefore it does not portray any one woman. She gives us the whole complex range of possibilities that occupy the vast reaches of the unconscious. The unconscious depths are a vital source and may be tapped by women according to their needs and inclinations. Enheduanna's poetry is an invitation to expand the definition of "woman" across the range her writing graphically depicts.

In the "Exaltation," Enheduanna is cruelly thrown out of her quarters

23. A baked-clay model of the ring-post symbol of Inanna from Uruk. Uruk period, c. 4000–3350 B.C.E. Courtesy of the Iraq Museum, Baghdad.

in the **gipar**. She loses her position, her status, her influence. However, she does not lose her voice. She remains steadfast in her convictions. She calls on professional chanters to sing her song in the broad light of day. She insists that Inanna keep her promise to protect and support the high priestess. Ultimately she is restored.

We offer thanks to Enheduanna for all her gifts and join her in exaltation:

> O maiden Inanna
> sweet is your praise

Notes

Notes to Chapter 1

1. Chapter titles in quotation marks are phrases from the poems to Inanna in Part 2 of the book.

2. Eric Neumann, *The Great Mother* (Princeton: Princeton University Press, 1955), 124.

3. Gertrude Rachel Levy, *The Gate of Horn* (London: Faber and Faber, 1948).

4. Diane Wolkstein and Samuel Noah Kramer, "Inanna: Queen of Heaven and Earth," in *Parabola* 5, no. 4 (1980), 86–89.

5. William W. Hallo and J. J. A. van Dijk, *The Exaltation of Inanna* (New Haven: Yale University Press, 1968).

6. In addition to *The Exaltation of Inanna*, endnote 5, for S. N. Kramer's translation of "Exalt" see "Hymnal Prayer of Enheduanna: The Adoration of Inanna in Ur," in James B. Pritchard, ed., *Ancient Near Eastern Texts Relating to the Old Testament*, 3rd ed. (Princeton: Princeton University Press, 1969) 579–582; translation of portions of "Exalt" by Anne Draffkorn Kilmer, "Inanna Exalted" in Joanna Bankier and Deirdre Lashgari, eds., *Women Poets of the World* (New York: Macmillan Publishing Co., 1983), 114–117; translation of "Exalt" in Aliki Barnstone and Willis Barnstone eds., *The Book of Women Poets: From Antiquity to Now* (New York: Shocken, 1992), 1–8, and a portion of the same poem in Jane Hirshfield, *Women in Praise of the Sacred* (New York: Harper Collins, 1994), 3–7. Also see Annette Zgoll, *Der Rechtsfall der En-hedu-Ana im Lied nin-me-\sara* (Münster: Ugarit-Verlag), 1997. For the poem "Lady of Largest Heart," see Åke W. Sjöberg, "A Hymn to the Goddess Inanna by the en-Priestess Enheduanna" in *Zeitschrift für Assyriologie* 65 (1975), 161–253. For "Inanna and Ebih," see B. L. Eichler, "in-nin me-huš-a" (edition of "Inanna and Ebih" in preparation, University of Pennsylvania, n.d.); S. N. Kramer reconstructed the text from various fragments; portions of his translation appear in *Sumerian Mythology* (New York: Harper & Row, 1961), 82–83. A French translation of "Inanna and Ebih" by S. N. Kramer appears in Jean Bottero and Samuel Noah Kramer, *Lorsque les dieux fai-*

saient l'homme (Paris: Gallimard, 1989), 219–229. A portion of "Ebih" was published by H. Limet, "Le poème épique 'Inina et Ebih': un version des lignes 123 à 182," *Orientalia* 40 (1971), 11–28.

7. Hallo and van Dijk, 9–10.

Notes to Chapter 2

1. The word "cunt" took on derogatory connotations in modern times. Deriving from the Indo-European base "Ku-," "cunt" is related to a variety of Germanic words meaning "a hollow space or place, an enclosing object, a round object, a lump," etc.; *kunt* or *kunte* meant vulva, and made its way into Middle English as *cunte*. See William Morris, ed., *The American Heritage Dictionary of the English Language* (Boston: Houghton Mifflin Company, 1978), 1524. Barbara Walker in *The Woman's Encyclopedia of Myths and Secrets* (San Francisco: Harper and Row, 1983), 197, says "cunt" is a "derivative of the Oriental Great Goddess as Cunti, or Kinda, the Yoni of the Uni-verse . . . also cunning, kenning, and ken: knowledge, learning, insight, remembrance, wisdom."

2. J. N. Postgate, *Early Mesopotamia* (London: Routledge, 1994), 54; and Krystyna Szarzynska, "Offerings for the Goddess Inanna in Archaic Uruk," *Revue d'Assyriologie* I (1993).

3. Beatrice Laura Goff, *Symbols of Prehistoric Mesopotamia* (New Haven: Yale University Press, 1963), 84.

4. Postgate, *Early,* 54.

5. Sumerian words in the text will be printed in bold to distinguish them from English.

6. Szarzynsk, 7.

7. Ibid., 8. S. N. Kramer (*Mythology,* 76) points out that the word **kur** [mountain] came to mean "foreign land," and then "land," in general. Its cosmic meaning is "nether world," probably its meaning in these ancient texts.

8. Ibid., 8–22.

9. Hans J. Nissen, *The Early History of the Ancient Near East* (Chicago: University of Chicago Press, 1988), 83.

10. Ibid., 105.

11. J. J. A. van Dijk, "Les contacts ethnique dans Mesopotamie," in Sven S. Hartman, ed., *Syncretism* (Stockholm: Almquist & Wiksell, 1969), 175 (translation of quotations my own).

12. Ibid., 176.

13. Ibid., 178.

14. Ibid., 174.

15. Simo Parpola, *Assyrian Prophecies* (Helsinki: Helsinki University Press, 1997), xxii and xxiii.

16. C. G. Jung, *Aion* (New York: Pantheon Books, 1959), 190, par. 189.

17. Piotr Michalowski, "Adapa and the Ritual Process" in *Rocznik Orientalistyczny,* T. XLI, Z. 2 (1980), 81.

18. Ibid.

19. Parpola, xxxiii.

20. Mark Glen Hall, "A Study of the Sumerian Moon-God, Nanna/Suen" (Ph.D. dissertation, University of Pennsylvania, 1985), 448.

21. Hallo and van Dijk, 49 and 48.

22. Parpola, xxvi.

23. C. G. Jung, *Mysterium coniunctionis* (New York: Pantheon Books, 1963), par. 760.

24. Samuel Noah Kramer, *Sumerian Mythology* (New York: Harper Torchbooks, 1961), 39–40.

25. Jung, *Aion*, par. 400.

26. Rivkah Harris, "Inanna-Ishtar as Paradox and a Coincidence of Opposites," *Journal of the History of Religions* 29 (1991), 267.

27. Ibid., 263.

28. C. G. Jung, *Psychology and Alchemy* (London: Routledge & Kegan Paul, 1953), par. 2.

29. Joan Goodnick Westenholz, "Love Lyrics from the Ancient Near East," in *Civilizations of the Ancient Near East,* Jack M. Sasson, ed., vol. IV. (New York: Charles Scribner's Sons, 1995), 2474.

30. Ibid., 2473–2474.

31. Samuel Noah Kramer, "The Temple in Sumerian Literature," in *Temple in Society,* Michael V. Fox, ed. (Winona Lake: Eisenbrauns, 1988), 15.

32. Ibid.

Notes to Chapter 3

1. Seton Lloyd, *The Archaeology of Mesopotamia* (London: Thames and Hudson, 1978), 22–25.

2. T. A. Muranaka, "Prehistoric 'Moods,'" *San Diego County Archeological Society Newsletter* (Sept./Oct. 1996), 4.

3. Charles Keith Maisels, *The Emergence of Civilization* (London: Routledge, 1990), 121.

4. Ibid., 121.

5. Joan Oates, "The Background and Development of Early Farming Communities in Mesopotamia and the Zagros, *Proceedings of the Prehistoric Society (London)* 39 (1973), 147–181, in Maisels, Ibid., 107 ff.

6. Maisels, 111.

7. Ibid.

8. Ibid., 160.

9. Joan Oates, "The Baked Clay Figurines from Tell Es-Sawwan," *Iraq* 28/2 (1966), 151.

10. Ibid., 147.

11. Maisels, 313.

12. Jeremy Black and Anthony Green, *Gods, Demons and Symbols of Ancient Mesopotamia* (Austin: University of Texas Press, 1992), 160.

13. Maisels, 114.

14. Marija Gimbutas, *The Language of the Goddess* (San Francisco: Harper Collins, 1989), 33 and throughout.

15. Robert McCormick Adams, *Heartland of Cities* (Chicago: University of Chicago Press, 1981), 59, in Maisels, 154.

16. Lloyd, 63.

17. Maisels, 114.

18. Joan Oates, "Ur and Eridu, the Prehistory," *Iraq* 20 (1960), 45.

19. Ibid., 46.

20. Rose Emily Rothenberg, "Psychic Wounds and Body Scars: an Exploration into the Psychology of Keloid Formation," *Spring* (1986), 141–154.

21. Henri Frankfort, "The Last Predynastic Period in Babylonia," *Cambridge Ancient History,* 3rd ed., vol. 1, part 2. I. E. S. Edwards, C. J. Gadd, N. G. L. Hammond, eds. (Cambridge: Cambridge University Press, 1971), 78.

22. Ibid., 79.

23. Nissen, 105–106.

24. I. J. Gelb, *A Study of Writing* (Berkeley: University of California Press, 1963), 62, quoted in Maisels, 138.

25. Thorkild Jacobsen, *Treasures of Darkness* (New Haven: Yale University Press, 1976), 77.

26. Denise Schmandt-Besserat, *Before Writing,* vol. I (Austin: University of Texas Press, 1992).

27. M. E. L. Mallowan, "The Early Dynastic Period in Mesopotamia," in *CAH*, vol. 1, 243–44.

28. Nissen, 135.

29. Mallowan, 278.

30. Maisels, 168–170.

31. Thorkild Jacobsen, *The Sumerian King List: Assyriological Studies* 11 (Chicago: Oriental Institute, 1939).

32. Enlil, also known as Lord Air, is thought to be of folk etymology. Because the meaning of Enlil's name is elusive, he may originally have been a non-Sumerian god.

Notes to Chapter 4

1. R. H. Dyson, Jr., "Sir Leonard Woolley and the Excavations at Ur," in Denise Schmandt-Besserat, *The Legacy of Sumer* (Malibu: Undena Publications, 1976), 121.

2. Ibid.

3. Irene J. Winter, "Women in Public: the Disc of Enheduanna, the Beginning of the Office of En-Priestess, and the Weight of Visual Evidence," in *La Femme dans le proche orient antique,* Jean-Marie Durand, ed. (Paris: Editions Recherché sur les Civilizations, 1987), 192. Winter notes that the inscription is "partly based upon an Old Babylonian copy" and argues that it "should be used only as a 'model' for the form of the inscription, not an exact copy."

4. Joan Goodnick Westenholz, "Enheduanna, En-Priestess, Hen of Nanna, Spouse of Nanna," in *Dumu é.dub.ba.a: Studies in Honor of Åke Sjöberg,* Hermann Behrens, Darlene Loding, and Martha Roth, eds. (Philadelphia: University of Pennsylvania Museum, 1989),

540. Westenholz does not think the hymn she titles "Love Dialogue between Nanna and Ningal" is the work of Enheduanna, although as she reports (550, fn. 52) "Wilcke suggests in Kollationen 47 that this text may have been composed by Enheduanna during her exile from Ur." See references for the Inanna hymns in endnote 5. The Temple Hymns, é-u₆-nir, are in Åke W. Sjöberg and E. Bergman, *Texts from Cuneiform Sources* (Locust Valley, New York: J. J. Augustin, 1969).

5. Sir Leonard Woolley, *Excavations at Ur* (London: Ernest Been, Ltd., 1954), 115.

6. Winter, 192, fn. 15.

7. Westenholz, 540.

8. Winter, 192.

9. Ibid., 193.

10. Ibid., 196, fn. 33.

11. Westenholz, 539.

12. Tikva Frymer-Kensky, *In the Wake of the Goddesses* (New York: The Free Press, 1992), 11. There were other apparent unifications of the Mesopotamian cities in the Early Dynastic period, but Sargon was the first to establish a new level of central government. See S. N. Kramer, *The Sumerians* (Chicago: University of Chicago Press, 1963), 43–60.

13. Oates, "Ur and Eridu," 46–47.

14. Postgate, *Early*, 41.

Notes to Chapter 5

1. William W. Hallo and William Kelly Simpson, *The Ancient Near East* (New York: Harcourt Brace, Jovanovitz, 1971), 55.

2. Sargon's mother's action accords with the evidence that priestesses were required to maintain chastity; however, some scholars believe priestesses could and did have children. We will discuss this controversy later.

3. Sargon's journey in a reed basket precedes that of Moses (Exodus 2: 1–10).

4. Brian Lewis, *The Sargon Legend: A Study of the Akkadian Text and the Tale of the Hero Who Was Exposed at Birth* in David Noel Freedman, ed., American Schools of Oriental Research Dissertation Series, no. 4.

5. C. J. Gadd, "The Dynasty of Agade and the Gutian Invasion," Edwards et al., *CAH*, vol. 1, part 2 (1971), 419.

6. Jerrold S. Cooper and Wolfgang Heimpel, "The Sumerian Sargon Legend," in *The Journal of the American Oriental Society*, 103:1 (January–March, 1983), 67–82.

7. Ibid., 76. Cooper and Heimple note: "Inana was the chief goddess of Kish, as she would be of Agade (as she was also of Lugalzagesi's Uruk) and thus on one level was the wife of the current king, Urzababa. The activity of Inana here on Sargon's behalf means that she is preparing to change royal husbands" (79, fn. 7).

8. Ibid., 78.

9. Ibid.

10. Ibid., 74.

11. Hallo and Simpson, 55.

12. Frymer-Kensky, 11.

13. Kramer, *Sumerians*, 58.

14. Ibid., 60–61.

15. Hallo and Simpson, 59.

16. Marija Gimbutas notes the existence of an Old European script that predates Sumerian cuneiform. See *Language*, 85.

17. Postgate, *Early*, 41.

18. Gadd, *CAH*, 446.

19. Postgate, *Early*, 41.

20. Maisels, 179.

21. Gadd, *CAH*, 450.

22. Maisels says that the Sargonic period was brought to an end "after that dynasty had overextended the cities' capabilities by continual warfare," ibid., 132.

Notes to Chapter 6

1. W. W. Hallo, "Gutium," *Reallexikon der Assyriologie*, 714.

2. Winter, 200–201.

3. Ibid., 201, fn. 44.

4. J. Renger, "Unterschungen zum Priestertum in der altababylonischen Zeit," *Zeitschrift für Assyriologie* 58 (1967), 132.

5. Hall, 889.

6. Ibid., 408.

7. Ibid., 33.

8. Ibid., 41.

9. Ibid., 42–45.

10. Westenholz, 544.

11. Hall, 99.

12. Weadock, 101. Also see E. Sollberger, "Sur la chronologie des rois d'Ur et quelques problèmes connexes," AfO 17 (1954/55), 24.

13. William W. Hallo, "Women of Sumer," in Denise Schmandt-Besserat, *The Legacy of Sumer* (Malibu: Undena Publications, 1976), 23.

14. Hall, 107.

15. Ibid., 226.

16. Maisels, 269.

17. Ibid., 297.

18. A. Falkenstein, "The Sumerian Temple City," monograph in *History: Ancient Near East* 1/1 (Los Angeles: Undena Publications, 1974), 7.

19. Ibid., 8.

20. Ibid.

21. Ibid.

22. Renger, 130.

23. At some point in the Sargonic period, the kings declared they owned the property

which formerly belonged to the temple. It is not clear whether this affected Enheduanna's authority over temple lands.

24. Winter, 190.

25. Edmond Sollberger, "Sur la chronologie des rois d'Ur et quelques problèmes connexes," *Archiv für Orientforschung* XVII/1 (1954/55), 26.

26. Alexander Marschack, *The Roots of Civilization* (New York: McGraw-Hill, 1972), 87.

27. Hall, 290.

28. Ibid., 538.

29. Ibid., 414.

30. Ibid., 316–317.

31. Ibid., 110.

32. Wolfgang Heimpel, "The Babylonian Background of the Term 'Milky Way,' " in Herman Behrens, Darlene Loding, and Martha Roth, eds., *Dumu é.dub.ba.a: Studies in Honor of Åke Sjöberg* (Philadelphia: University of Pennsylvania Museum, 1989), 249–252.

33. Penelope N. Weadock, "The *Giparu* at Ur," *Iraq, 37/2* (1975), 101.

34. Ibid., 116.

35. Hall, 730–731.

36. Weadock, 103.

37. Ibid.

38. H. H. Figulla, "Accounts Concerning Allocation of Provisions for Offerings in the Ningal-Temple at Ur," *Iraq* 15/1 (1953), 89 and 92.

39. Claus Wilke, 'Familiengründung in alten Babylonian," E. W. Muller, ed., *Geschlechtsreife und Legetimation zur Zeugung* (1985), 298, fn. 126. Thanks to Professor Anne D. Kilmer for this information.

40. Judy Grahn, *Blood, Bread, and Roses* (Boston: Beacon Press, 1993), 2–4, 11.

41. Jerrold S. Cooper, "Sacred Marriage and Popular Cult in Early Mesopotamia," Eíko Matsushima, ed., *Official Cult and Popular Religion in the Ancient Near East* (Heidelberg: Universitätsverlag C. Winter, 1993), 82–84.

42. Weadock, 118.

43. Ibid., 103.

44. Ibid., 117–118.

45. J. S. Cooper, "Heilige Hochzeit," *Reallexikon der Assyriologie,* vol. 4 (Berlin: Walter de Gruyter, 1972–1975), 260.

46. Douglas R. Frayne, "Notes on the Sacred Marriage Rite," *Bibliotheca Orientalis* XLII, no. 1–2 (Januari–Maart, 1985), 7.

47. Jacob Klein, "Shulgi of Ur: King of a Neo-Sumerian Empire," in *Civilizations of the Ancient Near East*, vol. 2, J. M. Sasson, ed. (New York: Charles Scribner's Sons, 1995), 847.

48. Cooper, "Sacred Marriage," 90.

49. Nissen, 105.

50. Renger, 134; C. J. Gadd, "En-An-E-Du," *Iraq* XIII, part I (1951), 32; H. W. F. Saggs, *The Greatness That Was Babylon,* (New York: Hawthorn Books, 1968), 333.

51. Lewis, 38.

52. Weadock, 102.
53. Hall, 405.
54. Ibid., 425.
55. Ibid., 426.
56. Frayne, 20–21.
57. Grahn, 17–18, 35–40, 89–93.
58. I. J. Gelb, A. L. Oppenheim, E. Reiner, et al., eds., *The Assyrian Dictionary of the Oriental Institute of the University of Chicago* (Gluckstadt/Locust Valley, N.Y.: J. J. Augustin, 1956), 84.
59. Hallo and van Dijk, 53.
60. Ibid.
61. Weadock, 122.
62. Ibid., 118.
63. Jacobsen, *Treasures,* 33.
64. J. Krecher, *Sumerische Kultlyrik* (Wiesbaden, 1966), 143.
65. Hallo and van Dijk, 59.
66. Ibid., 60.
67. Jacobsen, *Treasures,* 125.
68. Gadd, "En-An-E-Du," 39.
69. Hallo and van Dijk, 5.
70. Weadock, 103.
71. Ibid., 104.
72. Ibid., 109.

Notes to Chapter 7

1. Frymer-Kensky, 12.
2. Postgate, *Early,* 68.
3. Hall, 395.
4. Hallo and van Dijk, 4.
5. Sjöberg, 49. His translation of this verse is as follows:

> The compiler of the tablet (is) Enheduanna My lord, that which has been created (here) no one has created (before).

6. See Sjöberg, 5; Postgate, *Early,* 26: Hall, 398–399; Hallo and van Dijk, 3.
7. Sjöberg, 7.
8. Hall, 395.
9. Sjöberg, 5.
10. Hall, 398–399.
11. Hallo and van Dijk, 10.
12. Ibid., 8. Hallo and van Dijk say that in Uruk she would have served the god of heaven, An, and would have been "regarded as the virtual personification of Inanna."
13. Ibid., 4.

14. Nissen, 165.
15. Ibid.
16. Ibid., 178.
17. Ibid., 176.

Notes to Part II Introduction

1. Michael Fishbane, "Israel and the 'Mothers,' " in Peter L. Berger, ed., *The Other Side of God*, (Garden City: Anchor Press/Doubleday, 1981), 29. Fishbane says, "The cumulative evidence of ancient Near Eastern religions presents us with a fairly stable and certainly identifiable mythic structure. By this structure I have in mind a cosmos perceived as a plenum, interlocking and interconnected in substance. This substance is a unity—insofar as nature is perceived as an unbroken continuum pulsating with divine life. Indeed, it is the very power and vitality of the gods which constitutes this chain of natural being. The world is not merely the garment of the gods, it is also their very body and substance."

2. Frymer-Kensky, 71.

3. J. N. Postgate, *First Empires* (London: Phaidon Press Ltd., 1977), 12.

4. Kramer, *Sumerians*, 292 ff. for Kramer's comparison of fifteen parallels between biblical and Sumerian mythological and conceptual themes, including the creation of the universe and of man, paradise, the flood, and the idea of a personal god.

5. Ibid., 299.

6. Parpola, xxi, says, "The idea of God as 'the sum total of gods' is attested in various parts of the ancient Near East already in the sixth century bc, and later in several Hellenistic and Oriental philosophies and religions . . . It certainly also was part and parcel of first-millennium bc Jewish monotheism, as shown by the biblical designation of 'God,' *el\ohîm,* which literally means 'gods.' "

7. Fishbane, 32–35.

8. John A. Phillips, *Eve the History of an Idea* (San Francisco: Harper and Row, 1984), 12. Phillips says, "It is not incidental that the concept of nature, traditionally associated with goddesses, is totally absent in the Old Testament." He calls the creation language of Genesis the language of craftsmanship, not the language of nature.

9. Ibid., 38–39.

10. John R. Maier, "Charles Olson and the Poetic Uses of Mesopotamian Scholarship," *Journal of the American Oriental Society,* 103:1 (January–March, 1983), 228.

11. Ibid., 223.

12. Ibid., 230.

Notes to Chapter 8

1. Postgate, *Early,* 8.

2. J. V. Kinnier Wilson, *The Rebel Lands* (Cambridge: Cambridge University Press, 1979), 8.

3. M. B. Rowton, "Sumer's Strategic Periphery in Topological Perspective," in G. Van

Driel, Th. J. H. Krispijn, M. Stol, and K. R. Veenhof, eds., *Zikir Sumim: Assyriological Studies Presented to F. R. Kraus on the Occasion of his Seventieth Birthda*y (Leiden: E. J. Brill, 1982), 322.

4. Hallo and van Dijk, 3.

5. **"In-nin-me-huš-a"** is the first line of the poem and the traditional ancient Sumerian title, here translated as "Lady of blazing dominion." "Inanna and Ebih" is the common modern name of the poem.

6. The lapis net, **sa-za-gìn**, is related to the "great net," **sa-šuš-gal**, a weapon associated with "the wrath and power of the gods generally" according to Hall, 101.

7. The Sumerians were referred to as the "black-headed."

8. Inanna is older sister to the sun god, Utu.

9. Elam, Subir, and Lullubi were lands belonging to enemies of Sargon. Elam was east of Sumer. Subir was in the Kabur Plains and contained important cities in the third millennium. Lullubu lay between Elam and Subir in the mountains and was thought of as the place where barbarians lived.

10. The holy jump rope of Inanna is part of a game or dance that appears in her festivals.

11. Aratta was a mountain city in ancient Iran whose people worshiped the Sumerian pantheon, the principle deity of which was Inanna. Aratta was known for its supply of precious stones and excellent crafts. See Kramer, *Sumerians*, 274.

12. For comparison see Kramer's translation of these lines as follows (Kramer, *Mythology*, 83):

> The long spear I shall hurl upon it,
> The throw stick, the weapon, I shall direct against it
> At its neighboring forests I shall strike up fire,
> At its . . . I shall set up the bronze ax,
> All its waters like Gibil (the fire-god) the purifier
>   I shall dry up
> Like the mountain Aratta, I shall remove its dread,
> Like a city cursed by An, it sill not be restored
> Like (a city) on which Enlil frowns, it shall not
>   rise up

13. The word **ul** in this verse, "beauty" or "happiness," can also mean the bud of a flower.

14. The phrase **nam-šul-ak** in this verse refers to youthful male vigor, a young man in his prime, an example of Inanna's androgyny.

15. A term of respect for the male great gods.

16. The Sumerian word **silim** is related to the modern Hebrew greeting "Shalom," cognate to the Arabic "Salam" and to ancient Akkadian "Shulmu"; this Semitic expression, meaning "well being/be well," was borrowed into (non-Semitic) Sumerian as **silim**. (Thanks to Anne D. Kilmer for this information.)

17. The Sumerian word **an-ti-bal**, "pillars," means standing place, stand, or post, probably a celestial image, and is a symbol of royalty which cannot yet be identified.

18. The **muš-sag-kal** is a mythological creature, the first or primary or archetypal snake.

19. The Annuna are the council of the gods. Their name in Sumerian **a-nun-ke₄** means "water or semen of the prince" and probably derives from Enki, the earth god of sweet waters, god of wisdom, whose ejaculation in one myth creates the Tigris and Euphrates rivers.

20. Kramer's translation is as follows (*Mythology*, 83):

> Against the standing place of the gods it has directed its terror,
>> In the sitting place of the Annunaki it has led forth fearfulness,
> Its dreadful fear it has hurled upon the land,
>> The 'mountain,' its dreadful rays of fire it has directed against all the lands.

21. The **kurgarra** and the **gala** are priests of ambiguous gender. See the discussion under the heading "Androgyny" in the next poem "Lady of Largest Heart."

22. The ritual head-overturning ceremony is described fully in the comments on the next poem.

23. Enheduanna refers to the **me** of Inanna frequently. In this and the other poems, I have translated the Sumerian word **me** in various ways. The first line of "Ebih" could read "Lady of the blazing **me**." I have translated this line as "Lady of blazing dominion." In the final poem, "The Exaltation of Inanna," the first line "Queen of all given powers" could read "Queen of all the **me**." In "Ebih," Inanna reminds An of the generous portion of the **me** he gave to her. Enheduanna actually lists some of the **me** of Inanna in the next poem, "Lady of Largest Heart" (in the "are yours, Inanna" section), and in the final poem (in the "Proclaim" section).

24. See for example Patricia Reis, *Daughters of Saturn* (New York: Continuum, 1997).

25. Phillips, 41.

26. Genesis 3:5.

27. Carol Meyers translates this passage as follows:

> For to your man is your desire
> And he shall predominate over you.

See her *Discovering Eve* (New York: Oxford University Press, 1988), 118.

28. R. Graves and R. Patai, *Hebrew Myths: the Book of Genesis* (London: Cassell, 1964), 65.

29. Ibid., 66.

30. M. T. Colonna, "Lilith, of the Black Moon," *The Journal of Analytical Psychology* 25:4 (October, 1980), 326.

31. Meyers translates this portion of the text as follows:

> I will greatly increase your toil and your pregnancies
> (Along) with travail shall you beget children.

32. "The Descent of Inanna to the Underworld," in Betty De Shong Meador, *Uncursing the Dark* (Wilmette, Illinois: Chiron Publications, 1992).

Notes to Chapter 9

1. Åke W. Sjöberg, who translated this poem, reports that it appears "in the Old Babylonian literary catalogue AUAM 73.2302, I [in-nin] šà-gur₄-ra followed by [in-nin] me-huš-a ("Inanna and Ebih") and nin-me-šár-ra ("Exaltation"). Sjöberg, 166.

2. Jung, *Aion,* par. 267.

3. Parpola, xxi.

4. Ibid., xxi, fn. 21.

5. In-nin ša-gur₄-ra is the first line of this poem, translated here as "Lady of largest heart."

6. The term giš-hur, scratching with a piece of wood, is a theological notion that refers to a divine plan or design. Much later it became the diviner's magic circle.

7. Inanna has the power to shift one's perception, changing a friend into an enemy.

8. God of thunder.

9. The Sumerian word used here, la-la, refers to the handsomeness, appeal, vigor of a male.

10. Inanna names the woman pili-pili, a name that refers to certain temple personnel, usually male. Sjöberg understands this passage to refer to a changing of the role of the woman to that of a man (Sjöberg, 226). Henshaw disagrees, saying he finds no evidence for this idea (Henshaw, 299). The head-overturning rite, sag-šu-bal, in which Inanna changes woman into man, man into woman is documented in other literary texts. In "Ebih" Inanna performs the head-overturning rite for the personnel in her new temple. Sjöberg mentions a number of other texts in which Inanna changes man into woman, woman into man (Sjöberg, 223–226), a power attributed to Inanna in this poem in the "are yours" section. The pili-pili and the kurgarra are female and male temple personnel who have undergone this rite. In this poem they are ecstatic priestess and priest, lú-al-è-dè.

11. Hallo and van Dijk, 3, translate this phrase " 'tis thine," and accord this section particular importance saying, "its principle theme is acknowledgment of Inanna's jurisdiction, her omnipresent and omnipotent role in human affairs under the motto of ' 'tis thine.' "

12. This line begins me téš which has the meaning of modesty or a quality barbarians do not possess. The me in the phrase could identify the "modesty" as a divine quality, one of the me. The Akkadian inter-linear translation uses the words du-tam ba-áš-tam as equivalent, a moral quality, a protective life force or spirit which guards virility. The derivative verb in Akkadian means shame. A related word in Hebrew, bōš, means shame as well as menstrual cloth; both have very negative connotations.

13. Note this section's parallel with the gnostic "Thunder, Perfect Mind (VI, 2)" in Marvin W. Meyer, ed., *The Nag Hammadi Library* (New York: Harper & Row, 1977), 271, another document based on paradoxical opposites. The last two verses of the "are yours" are echoed in "Thunder":

> For many are the sweet forms which exist in numerous
> sins and incontinences, and disgraceful passions
> And fleeting pleasures; which people embrace,
> Until they become sober and go up to their place

of rest
And they will find me there,
and live, and not die again.
Quoted in Parpola, xxxiv.

Parpola agrees with G. Quespel's suggestion that the speaker in "Thunder" is Anat, viz. Ishtar/Inanna or Isis, saying of the speaker "as the coincidence of opposites, the power of love joining the opposites and governing them all," fn. 130, XCV.

14. In a transliteration, the language scholar writes in Latin characters the words depicted in cuneiform script on the original tablet.

15. In transliterating Sumerian texts, "x" indicates a broken sign; letters or words in square brackets indicate broken signs that have been restored. Capitalized letters or words indicate probable readings.

16. These quotes are from notes taken during studies with Foxvog.

17. Sjöberg, 183.

18. Ibid.

19. Ibid., 181.

20. Ibid., 183.

21. Marschack, 136.

22. Chris Knight, *Blood Relations: Menstruation and the Origins of Culture* (New Haven: Yale University Press, 1991), 283.

23. Ibid., 46 (emphasis in text).

24. Grahn throughout her book compiles common elements of menstrual rituals reported in various sources from around the world. See Chapter 6.

25. Ibid., 32.

26. Diane Wolkstein and Samuel Noah Kramer, *Inanna Queen of Heaven and Earth* (New York: Harper and Row, 1983), 95–96.

27. Knight, 213 and 249. That women closely associated synchronize their menstrual periods was scientifically demonstrated in the 1970s. Knight says that if women need to "phase-lock themselves to a lunar schedule" they can easily accomplish this task.

28. The number seven is numinous throughout the ancient Near East, occurring in Hebrew mythology, for example, as Yahweh created the earth in seven days.

29. Wolkstein and Kramer, 170.

30. Parpola, xxxiii, fn. 130.

31. In the Sumerian text "Enki and the World Order" all the gods and goddesses except Inanna are given realms of duty/power by Enki. Inanna complains of this to Enki, and in the text "Inanna and the God of Wisdom," she takes the **me** from the drunken Enki, escaping to her home port in Uruk.

32. This ax that Inanna uses to smash heads is called "the devourer" or "the eater."

33. Parpola, xxvi.

34. Harris, 269.

35. Parpola, xv.

36. Wolkstein and Kramer, 170.

37. Gadd, "Agade," 453.

38. Richard A. Henshaw, *Female and Male* (Allison Park, Pennsylvania: Pickwick Publications, 1994), 236.

39. From my rendition of tablet Ni 9602, column iii, reverse.

40. Parpola, xxxi and fn. 120.

41. Will Roscoe, "Priests of the Goddess: Gender Transgression in Ancient Religion," *History of Religions,* vol. 35, no. 3 (February, 1996), 213.

42. Henshaw, 225 and 226.

43. Ibid., 197.

44. Ibid., 191.

45. Anne Draffkorn Kilmer, "An Oration on Babylon," *Altorientalische Forschungen* 18:1 (1991), 11.

46. Henshaw, 217. The King List is part fable, part historical chronology of Kings in the Early Dynastic period. See Jacobsen, *King List.*

47. Paula Gunn Allen, "Beloved Women: Lesbians in American Indian Cultures," *Conditions* 7 (1981), 81, quoted in Judy Grahn, *Another Mother Tongue* (Boston: Beacon Press, 1984), 62.

48. Ibid., 48.

49. Mircea Eliade, *The Two and the One* (Chicago: University of Chicago Press, 1979), 113, in Harris, 277.

50. Roscoe, 203. Roscoe cites Tertullian. *Ad nationes,* 1.20.4; *Scriptores historiae Augustae, Alexander Severus,* 23.7; Prudentius, *Peristephanon,* 10.1071.

51. Roscoe, 204.

52. Kilmer, "Oration," 16.

53. Harris, 265.

54. Henshaw, 284.

55. Ibid., 289–290.

56. Dietz Otto Edzard, "Zur Ritualfel Der Son. 'Love Lyrics,'" in *Festschrift for E. Reiner,* (AOS 67, 1987), 58.

57. Henshaw, 298.

58. Roscoe, 214.

59. Parpola, xlvi.

Notes to Chapter 10

1. "The Exaltation of Inanna" is the modern title taken from Hallo and van Dijk. The ancient title would have been the first line of the poem **nin-me-šár-a.**

2. Hallo and van Dijk elaborate on Inanna as deity of heaven and earth: "the comparison with heaven and earth implies at the same time the combination of astral and terrestrial character peculiar to the goddess in later descriptions. Here, in fact, is the historical point at which these two contradictory characterizations are first united in the one deity. She owes her astral nature (as the planet Venus) to Ištar; but her claim to the role of earth goddess is based on her identification, as Inanna, with Antum=ki, the terrestrial consort of the Heaven-god," 60–61.

3. Parpola, xlv. "The Neo-Assyrian term for 'prophet' . . . literally means 'shouter/proclaimer.' Such a term immediately reminds one of John the Baptist, 'the shouting one,' and of his ninth century B.C.E. predecessor, Elijah . . ."

4. Here again Inanna is associated with the ecstatic while also being identified with the crescent horns of the wild cow, a symbol of Nanna's new moon crescent.

5. See endnote 16, Chapter 8.

6. Another name for Inanna's consort Dumuzi.

7. Hallo and van Dijk, 53, say **nin-banda**, minor queen, "is almost certainly a courtly title in the human sphere . . . 'little queen,' second queen, princess." Enheduanna herself may have had this title earlier as princess in the household of Sargon.

8. The holy tavern is a divine brothel. Inanna is goddess of prostitutes and sexual love. See Kramer, *Mythology,* 86; Parpola, xxxi.

9. Kramer in Pritchard, 582, translates this verse, "It is because of your captive spouse, your captive son," and in a footnote says "This probably refers to some disaster in Erech." Hallo and van Dijk, 33, translate, "(Only) on account of your captive spouse, on account of your captive child, / Your rage is increased, your heart unassuaged." In the context of the poem I have interpreted this to mean that Inanna's heart is unassuaged because her devoted Enheduanna is in captivity. Hallo and van Dijk appear to make that interpretation also.

10. Hallo and van Dijk, 3, say of this event, "There can be little doubt that this is simply a hymnic expansion of the same acknowledgment that, according to the historical tradition, marked Sargon's successful suppression of the general rebellion late in his reign."

11. Ibid., 9.

12. Nissen, 172.

13. Hallo and van Dijk, 61.

14. Ibid., 62.

15. Ibid., 57.

16. Hallo and van Dijk, 59.

17. Parpola, xxxiv.

18. Roscoe, 228.

19. Parpola, xxxiv.

20. Marie-Louise von Franz, *C. G. Jung—His Myth in Our Time* (New York: G. P. Putnam's Sons, 1975), 19.

21. David Biale, "The God with Breasts," *History of Religions,* 20:3 (February, 1982), 253.

22. Roscoe, 227–228.

23. In the United States in the past two decades women across the country have responded to the search for a female-oriented spirituality, and a body of literature has developed out of this spontaneous movement. See the works of Lucia Birnbaum, Jean Shinoda Bolin, Janine Canan, Carol Christ, Diane di Prima, Christine Downing, Elinor Gadon, Marija Gimbutas, Judith Gleason, Judy Grahn, Nor Hall, Linda Leonard, Sylvia Perera, Virginia Rutter, Charlene Spretnak, Starhawk, Merlin Stone, Barbara Walker, and many others. These texts and the additional publications, rituals, and workshops spawned by the search for opportunities to explore spirituality have provided women a sense of place

outside traditional religion. Nevertheless, each woman has to find the right environment for her own spiritual growth.

24. Hallo and van Dijk, 54–55, attest that the ritual basket carried grain. The shout of joy, like the grain, pertains to Enheduanna's role in assuring fertility.

25. Ibid., 4–5.

26. Parpola, xxxviii.

27. Ibid., xxxix.

28. Ibid., 39.

29. See for example Merlin Stone, *When God Was a Woman* (San Diego: Harcourt Brace, 1976); Anne Baring and Jules Cashford, *The Myth of the Goddess* (New York: Viking, 1991); Elinor Gadon, *The Once and Future Goddess* (New York: Harper, 1989); Alicia Suskin Ostriker, *Feminist Revision and the Bible* (Oxford: Blackwell, 1993).

Bibliography

Adams, Robert McCormick. *Heartland of Cities*. Chicago: University of Chicago Press, 1981. Quoted in Charles Maisels, *The Emergence of Civilization*. London: Routledge, 1990.

Allen, Paula Gunn. "Beloved Women: Lesbians in American Indian Cultures." *Conditions* 7 (1981). Quoted in Judy Grahn, *Another Mother Tongue*. Boston: Beacon Press, 1984.

Baring, Anne and Jules Cashford. *The Myth of the Goddess*. New York: Viking, 1991.

Barnstone, Aliki and Willis Barnstone, eds. *The Book of Women Poets: From Antiquity to Now*. New York: Shocken, 1992.

Biale, David. "The God with Breasts." *History of Religions* 20, no. 3 (February, 1982).

Black, Jeremy and Anthony Green. *Gods, Demons and Symbols of Ancient Mesopotamia*. Austin: University of Texas Press, 1992.

Bottero, Jean and Samuel Noah Kramer. *Lorsque les dieux faisaient L'homme*. Paris: Gallimard, 1989.

Colonna, M. T. "Lilith, or the Black Moon." *The Journal of Analytical Psychology* 25, no. 4 (October, 1980).

Cooper, Jerrold S. "Heilige Hochziet." *Reallexikon der Assyriologie* 4. Berlin: Walter de Gruyter, 1972–1975.

_____. "Sacred Marriage and Popular Cult in Early Mesopotamia." In *Official Cult and Popular Religion in the Ancient Near East*. Heidelberg: Universitätsverlag C. Winter, 1993.

Cooper, Jerrold S. and Wolfgang Heimpel. "The Sumerian Sargon Legend." *The Journal of the American Oriental Society* 103, no. 1 (January–March, 1983).

Dyson, R. H. Jr. "Sir Leonard Woolley and the Excavations at Ur." In *The Legacy of Sumer*, edited by Denise Schmandt-Besserat. Malibu: Undena Publications, 1976.

Edzard, Dietz Otto. "Zur Ritualfel Der Son. 'Love Lyrics.'" In *Festschrift for E. Reiner*. *Journal of the American Oriental Society* 67 (1987).

Eichler, B. L. "in-nin me-huš-a." In preparation, University of Pennsylvania, n.d.

Eliade, Mircea. *The Two and the One*. Chicago: University of Chicago Press, 1979.
   Quoted in Rivkah Harris, "Inanna/Ishtar as Paradox and Coincidence of
   Opposites," *Journal of the History of Religions* 29 (1991).

Falkenstein, A. *Archaische Texte aus Uruk,* Ausgrabungen der Deutschen
   Forschungsgemeinschaft in *Uruk-Warka,* 2 (Berlin: Deutsche
   Forschungsgemeinschaft, 1936), Zeichenliste, fig. 208.

————. "The Sumerian Temple City." Monograph in *History: Ancient Near East* 1,
   no. 1. Los Angeles: Undena Publications, 1974.

Figulla, H. H. "Accounts Concerning Allocation of Provisions for Offerings in the
   Ningal-Temple at Ur." *Iraq* 15, no. 1 (1953).

Fishbane, Michael. "Israel and the 'Mothers.' " In *The Other Side of God*, edited by
   Peter L. Berger. Garden City: Anchor Press/Doubleday, 1981.

Frankfort, Henri. "The Last Predynastic Period in Babylonia." In *Cambridge Ancient
   History*. Vol. 1, Part 2. I. E. S. Edwards, C. J. Gadd, and N. G. L. Hammond, eds.
   Cambridge: Cambridge University Press, 1971.

Frymer-Kensky, Tikva. *In the Wake of the Goddesses*. New York: The Free Press, 1992.

Frayne, Douglas R. "Notes on the Sacred Marriage Rite." *Bibliotheca Orientalis* 42,
   no. 1–2 (Januari–Maart, 1985).

Gadd, C. J. "En-An-E-Du." *Iraq* 13, Part 1 (1951).

————. "The Dynasty of Agade and the Gutian Invasion." In *Cambridge Ancient
   History*. Vol. 1, Part 2. I. E. S. Edwards, C. J. Gadd, and N. G. L. Hammond, eds.
   Cambridge: Cambridge University Press, 1971.

Gadon, Elinor W. *The Once and Future Goddess*. New York: Harper, 1989.

Gelb, I. J. *A Study of Writing*. Berkeley: University of California Press, 1963.

Gelb, I. J., A. L. Oppenheim, E. Reiner, et al., eds. *The Assyrian Dictionary of the
   Oriental Institute of the University of Chicago*. Gluckstadt/Locust Valley, New
   York: J. J. Augustin, 1956.

Gimbutas, Marija. *The Language of the Goddess*. San Francisco: Harper Collins, 1989.

Goff, Beatrice Laura. *Symbols of Prehistoric Mesopotamia*. New Haven: Yale University
   Press, 1963.

Grahn, Judy. *Blood, Bread, and Roses*. Boston: Beacon Press, 1993.

Graves, R. and R. Patai. *Hebrew Myths: the Book of Genesis*. London: Cassell, 1964.

Hall, Mark Glen. "A Study of the Sumerian Moon-God, Nanna/Suen." Ph.D.
   dissertation, University of Pennsylvania, 1985.

Hallo, William W. "Gutium." *Reallexikon der Assyriologie*.

————. "Women of Sumer." In *The Legacy of Sumer*, edited by Denise
   Schmandt-Besserat. Malibu: Undena Publications, 1976.

Hallo, William W. and J. J. A. van Dijk. *The Exaltation of Inanna*. New Haven: Yale
   University Press, 1968.

Hallo, William W. and William Kelly Simpson. *The Ancient Near East*. New York:
   Harcourt Brace, Jovanovitz, 1971.

Harris, Rivkah. "Inanna-Ishtar as Paradox and a Coincidence of Opposites." *Journal of
   the History of Religions* 29 (1991).

Heimpel, Wolfgang. "The Babylonian Background of the Term 'Milky Way.' " In *Dumu é.dub.ba.a: Studies in Honor of Åke Sjöberg*, edited by Herman Behrens, Darlene Loding, and Martha Roth, 249-252. Philadelphia: University of Pennsylvania Museum, 1989.

Henshaw, Richard A. *Female and Male*. Allison Park, Pennsylvania: Pickwick Publications, 1994.

Hirshfield, Jane. *Women in Praise of the Sacred*. New York: Harper Collins, 1994.

Jacobsen, Thorkild. *The Sumerian King List: Assyriological Studies 11*. Chicago: Oriental Institute, 1939.

_____. *Treasures of Darkness*. New Haven: Yale University Press, 1976.

Jung, C. G. *Psychology and Alchemy*. London: Routledge & Kegan Paul, 1953.

_____. *Aion*. New York: Pantheon Books, 1959.

_____. *Mysterium coniunctionis*. New York: Pantheon Books, 1963.

Kilmer, Anne Draffkorn. "Inanna Exalted." In *Women Poets of the World*, edited by Joanna Bankier and Deirdre Lashgari. New York: Macmillan Publishing Co., 1983.

_____. "An Oration on Babylon." *Altorientalische Forschungen*. Vol. 18, no. 1 (1991).

Klein, Jacob. "Shulgi of Ur: King of a Neo-Sumerian Empire." In *Civilizations of the Ancient Near East*. Vol. 2, edited by J. M. Sasson. New York: Charles Scribner's Sons, 1995.

Knight, Chris. *Blood Relations: Menstruation and the Origins of Culture*. New Haven: Yale University Press, 1991.

Kramer, Samuel Noah. *The Sumerians*. Chicago: University of Chicago Press, 1963.

_____. "Hymnal Prayer of Enheduanna: The Adoration of Inanna in Ur." In *Ancient Near Eastern Texts Relating to the Old Testament*. 3rd ed., edited by James B. Pritchard. Princeton: Princeton University Press, 1969.

_____. *Sumerian Mythology*. New York: Harper & Row, 1961.

_____. "The Temple in Sumerian Literature." In *Temple in Society*, edited by Michael V. Fox. Winona Lake: Eisenbrauns, 1988.

Krecher, J. *Sumerische Kultlyrik*. Wiesbaden, 1966.

Levy, Gertrude Rachel. *The Gate of Horn*. London: Faber and Faber, 1948.

Lewis, Brian. *The Sargon Legend: A Study of the Akkadian Text and the Tale of the Hero Who Was Exposed at Birth*. In American Schools of Oriental Research Dissertation Series, no. 4, edited by David Noel Freedman, 1980.

Limet, H. "Le poème épique 'Inina et Ebih': un version des lignes 123 à 182." *Orientalia* 40 (1971).

Lloyd, Seton. *The Archaeology of Mesopotamia*. London: Thames and Hudson, 1978.

Maier, John R. "Charles Olson and the Poetic Uses of Mesopotamian Scholarship." *Journal of the American Oriental Society* 103, no. 1 (January–March, 1983).

Maisels, Charles Keith. *The Emergence of Civilization*. London: Routledge, 1990.

Mallowan, M. E. L. "The Early Dynastic Period in Mesopotamia." In *Cambridge Ancient History*. Vol. 1, Part 2. I. E. S. Edwards, C. J. Gadd, and N. G. L. Hammond eds. Cambridge: Cambridge University Press, 1971.

Marschack, Alexander. *The Roots of Civilization.* New York: McGraw-Hill, 1972. Revised edition, 1991.

Meador, Betty De Shong. *Uncursing the Dark.* Wilmette, Illinois: Chiron Publications, 1992.

Meyers, Carol. *Discovering Eve.* New York: Oxford University Press, 1988.

Michalowski, Piotr. "Adapa and the Ritual Process." *Rocznik Orientalistyczny* T. 41, Z. 2 (1980).

Morris, William, ed. *The American Heritage Dictionary of the English Language.* Boston: Houghton Mifflin Company, 1978.

Muranaka, T. A. "Prehistoric 'Moods.' " *San Diego County Archeological Society Newsletter* (Sept./Oct. 1996): 4.

Neumann, Eric. *The Great Mother.* Princeton: Princeton University Press, 1955.

Nissen, Hans J. *The Early History of the Ancient Near East.* Chicago: University of Chicago Press, 1988.

Oates, Joan. "Ur and Eridu, the Prehistory." *Iraq* 20 (1960).

————. "The Baked Clay Figurines from Tell Es-Sawwan." *Iraq* 28, no. 2 (1966).

————. "The Background and Development of Early Farming Communities in Mesopotamia and the Zagros." *Proceedings of the Prehistoric Society (London)* 39 (1973): 147–81. Quoted in Charles Maisels, *The Emergence of Civilization.* London: Routledge, 1990.

Ostriker, Alicia Suskin. *Feminist Revision and the Bible.* Oxford: Blackwell, 1993.

Parpola, Simo. *Assyrian Prophecies.* Helsinki: Helsinki University Press, 1997.

Phillips, John A. *Eve the History of an Idea.* San Francisco: Harper and Row, 1984.

Postgate, J. N. *The First Empires.* London: Phaidon Press Ltd., 1977.

————. *Early Mesopotamia.* London: Routledge, 1994.

Reis, Patricia. *Daughters of Saturn.* New York: Continuum, 1997.

Renger, J. "Unterschungen zum Priestertum in der altababylonischen Zeit." *Zeitschrift für Assyriologie* 58 (1967).

Rothenberg, Rose Emily. "Psychic Wounds and Body Scars: an Exploration into the Psychology of Keloid Formation." *Spring* (1986).

Roscoe, Will. "Priests of the Goddess: Gender Transgression in Ancient Religion." *History of Religions* 35, no. 3 (February, 1996).

Rowton, M. B. "Sumer's Strategic Periphery in Topological Perspective." In *Zikir Sumim: Assyriological Studies Presented to F. R. Kraus on the Occasion of His Seventieth Birthday,* edited by G. Van Driel, Th. J. H. Krispijn, M. Stol, and K. R. Veenhof. Leiden: E. J. Brill, 1982.

Saggs, H. W. F. *The Greatness That Was Babylon.* New York: Hawthorn Books, 1962.

Schmandt-Besserat, Denise. *Before Writing.* Vol. I. Austin: University of Texas Press, 1992.

Sjöberg, Åke W. "A Hymn to the Goddess Inanna by the en-Priestess Enheduanna." *Zeitschrift fur Assyriologie* 65 (1975): 161–253.

Sjöberg, Åke and E. Bergman. *Texts from Cuneiform Sources.* Locust Valley, New York: J. J. Augustin, 1969.

Sollberger, Edmond. "Sur la chronologie des rois d'Ur et quelques problèmes
connexes." *Archiv für Orientforschung* 17, no. 1 (1954/55).

Stone, Merlin. *When God Was a Woman.* San Diego: Harcourt Brace, 1976.

Szarzynska, Krystyna. "Offerings for the Goddess Inanna in Archaic Uruk." *Revue
d'Assyriologie* 1, (1993): 7–29.

van Dijk, J. J. A. "Les contacts ethnique dans Mesopotamie." In *Syncretism,* edited by
Sven S. Hartman. Stockholm: Almqvist & Wiksell, 1969.

von Franz, Marie-Louise. *C. G. Jung—His Myth in Our Time.* New York: G. P.
Putnam's Sons, 1975.

Walker, Barbara. *The Woman's Encyclopedia of Myths and Secrets.* San Francisco: Harper
and Row, 1983.

Weadock, Penelope N. "The *Giparu* at Ur." *Iraq* 37, no. 2 (1975).

Westenholz, Joan Goodnick. "Enheduanna, En-Priestess, Hen of Nanna Spouse of
Nanna." In *Dumu é.dub.ba.a: Studies in Honor of Åke Sjöberg,* edited by Hermann
Behrens, Darlene Loding, and Martha Roth. Philadelphia: University of
Pennsylvania Museum, 1989.

_____. "Love Lyrics from the Ancient Near East." In *Civilizations of the Ancient
Near East.* Volume 4, edited by Jack M. Sasson. New York: Charles Scribner's
Sons, 1995.

Wilke, Claus. "Familiengründung in alten Babylonian." In *Geschlechtsreife und
Legetimation zur Zeugung,* edited by E. W. Muller (1985).

Wilson, J. V. Kinnier. *The Rebel Lands.* Cambridge: Cambridge University Press, 1979.

Winter, Irene J. "Women in Public: the Disc of Enheduanna, the Beginning of the Office
of En-Priestess, and the Weight of Visual Evidence." In *La Femme dans le proche
orient antique,* edited by Jean-Marie Durand. Paris: Editions Recherché sur les
Civilizations, 1987.

Wolkstein, Diane and Samuel Noah Kramer. "Inanna Queen of Heaven and Earth."
Parabola 5, no. 4 (1980).

_____. *Inanna: Queen of Heaven and Earth.* New York: Harper and Row, 1983.

Woolley, Sir Leonard. *Excavations at Ur.* London: Ernest Been, Ltd., 1954.

Zgoll, Annette. *Der Rechtsfall der En-hedu-Ana im Lied nin-me-šár-ra.* Münster:
Ugarit-Verlag, 1997.

Index

Note: As in the text, Sumerian words are set in **boldface** type; illustrations are denoted by page numbers in *italics*.

Abraham, 4

Abu Salabikh, literary text found at, 69

Ada (Enheduanna's steward), 52

Adam, 85, 109, 110, 111, 112

Adams, Robert, 28

Agade, 44, 47, 155, 185, 197n.7 (ch. 5)

Agade period, 158

agriculture, origins of, 25

Akkad, 42; Dynasty, 74; god of, 9, 48, 52, 185; language of, 41, 46, 50, 56; Sargon and, 8, 41, 46. *See also* Agade; Ishtar

alienation, origins of, 85–86

Allen, Paula Gunn, 162

al-'Ubaid. *See* Ubaid culture

American Indian culture, androgyny in, 162

Anat, 204–205n.13

androgyny, 204n.9; as bridge between heaven and earth, 162–163, 164; ceremonial, 162–167; Inanna's, 20, 202n.14; of temple attendants, 20, 102, 115–116, 162–163, 164; women

and, 123, 151, 162–167. *See also* **kurgarra**

An (god of Heaven), 34, 117, 122, 135, 171; as afraid, 143; betrayal of Inanna by, 85, 89, 97–99, 105, 106; collapse of, 125–126, 143, 183–184; defilement of, 175–176, 183–184; as dependent on nature, 184; disbursement of **me** by, 105, 142; Inanna and, 95, 178; as Inanna's great-grandfather, 16; marriage of, to Inanna, 17, 133; origins of, 16, 18; prayer to, 75, 176; Sargon and, 44; temples of, 50, 183

animals, as manifestations of goddesses, 83

Annuna (council of the gods), 203n.19; collapse of, 98, 106, 142, 143; Inanna and, 96, 117, 123, 125, 137, 151, 172–173, 177

Aqqi (Sargon's adoptive father), 43

Aratta, 94, 97, 202n.11

archetype, sacred, 165

architecture, developments in, 26

Inanna's spouse), 19, 58–59, 65, 161, 177, 207n.6

Dynasty, Third. *See* Ur III period

Eanna, 13–14, 30

Early Dynastic period: depictions of rank during, 40; empire building during, 103–104; end of, 33, 46; government in, 32; King List, 161, 206n.46; marriage ritual in, 58; office of priestess during, 49; plaque from, *14*; Sargon and, 41; Sumerian kings during, 43; temple **gipar** in, 64

Ebabber Temple, 70

Ebih (mountain), 89, 96; destruction of, 96, 99–101, 126, 172, 173; as paradise, 85, 98–99, 104–105, 183. *See also* "Inanna and Ebih"

economics, of the temple, 52, 53

ecstasy, spiritual, 163, 166, 204n.10, 207n.4

Edzard, D. O., 164

é-gal: as large household, 26, 33, 34, 51; as temple, 51, 70

Ekishnugal (temple), 72

Elam, 47, 93, 202n.9

"Elevation of Inanna" (poem), 17

Eliade, Mircea, 162

Elijah, 207n.3

emasculation, purpose of, 184, 186

emotion, perceptions of, 77, 150

en, as title for priests, 33

Enanedu (high priestess), 67

Enheduanna: appointment of, 41, 42, 47, 49, 181; as bride of Inanna, 77–78, 179, 188; as bridge between god and man, 42; as child of Inanna, 179, 188; devotion of, to Inanna, 6–7, 42, 77–78, 133–136, 187–188; discovery of, 8; elevation of Inanna by, 7, 35, 48, 73, 85, 90, 104, 113, 115, 142, 178–179, 180; exile of, 74–76, 77, 85, 155, 169, 177, 179, 183, 190–191, 196–197n.4,

207n.9; functions of, 52, 55–56, 63; identity of, 42, 48, 168–169; imagery used by, 19, 29, 70, 145, 170; influence of, 50–51, 66–67, 69, 71, 73, 155; life of, 32, 43, 45–46, 47; as a model of womanhood, 186; motivation for poetry of, 147–151; overthrow of, 174–175, 178, 181–183; personal integration of, 9; as poet, 6, 19, 37, 48, 155, 169–170; poetry of, 11–12, 23, 67, 68, 76–77, 155; portrait of, 37, 38–39, *38*, *39*, 40, 150–151; as priestess, 6, 40, 49, 50–51, 133, 139, 151, 155, 174, 186, 208n.24; psychology of, 86, 90; restoration of, 180, 191; Sargon and, 8, 42, 43; stature of, 73, 200n.12; suffering of, at Inanna's hands, 114, 125, 134, 169; theology of, 51, 73, 78–79, 114, 146–147; title of, 207n.7; as a warrior woman, 154–155; as wife of Nanna, 41, 42, 50, 55, 133; as a writer, 45, 69, 168–169

Enki (god of wisdom and sweet waters), 35, 203n.19; as creator of androgynes, 163; exile of, 66; **me** of, 17, 205n.31; temple of, 29

"Enki and the World Order," 205n.31

Enlil (god of the air; Lord Air), 35, 125, 196n.32; Inanna and, 15, 101, 118, 135, 172; powers of, 17, 94, 97, 176; Sargon and, 44

Enmerkar, king, 58

Ennatum, of Lagash, 8

Ennigaldi-Nanna, 64

en-priestess, 49, 50, 51, 52, 61

en-priests, 49, 50

epic. *See* "Gilgamesh, . . ."

epics, 16, 33, 56

Ereshkigal (Queen of the Underworld), 17

Eridu, temples at, 29, 155

etymology, 56, 61, 159, 163, 194n.1, 202nn.13,16, 204n.6

Eve, 85, 109, 110, 111, 112, 151
evil, as estrangement, 85–86
Exaltation of Inanna, The (Hallo and van
 Dijk), 6
"Exaltation of Inanna, The" (poem), 6,
 40, 42, 69, 77, 79, 85, 161, 168–191,
 206n.1
exile. *See* Enheduanna, exile of
eye(s): "coffee-bean," 26; snake, *39;*
 symbol of the single, 28; veiled, 62

Falkenstein, A., 52
Fara period, 56
fear, archaic, 146
fertility: focus of religion as, 158–159;
 goddesses of, 83, 104; as purpose of
 sacred marriage, 57, 58, 61, 160–161
festival, new moon, 53
figurines: Halaf, 27–28, *28;* Jarmo,
 24, *25;* lizard-headed, 26; male, 26;
 Sawwan, 26; snake-headed, 29–30, *30*
fire. *See* Gibil
flood, great, 33, 90
Foxvog, Daniel A., 5–6, 86–87, 137
Frankfort, Henri, 30
Franz, Marie Louise von, 185
Frayne, Douglas, 62
Frazer, James, 57
Frymer-Kensky, Tikva, 68

Gadd, C. J., 46, 47, 158
gala. *See* **galaturra**
galaturra (gala), 102, 163, 203n.21
galli, as the third sex, 163
Garden of Eden, Ebih as, 90
Gate of Horn (Levy), 4
gender, ambiguity of, 20, 162–167, 186,
 203n.21, 204n.9
gender-crossing, 162–163
gesture, symbolic, 40
Gibil (fire god), 93, 97
"Gilgamesh, Enkidu, and the Nether
 World," 16, 33

Gimbutas, Marija, 28, 198n.22 (ch. 5)
gipar, 64–65, *64,* 165; plaque from, *14.*
 See also high priestess, residence of
Gishbanda (god), 72
Gnosticism, 156, 157, 160, 204n.13. *See
 also* Sophia
goddess, 201n.8; of abundant harvest, 4;
 diminishing role of, 109; as dominant,
 83–84, 104, 184; figurines of, from
 Jarmo, 24, *25;* mother, 151; as proto-
 types of women, 56; snake-headed, 8,
 83; worship, 158, 189–190
godhead, female aspect of, 10, 156
god(s): as distinct from nature, 105, 107;
 of the herds, 50; hierarchy of, 51; as
 individuals, 74–76; intimacy of, with
 humans, 148, 187; male, 34–35, 84–
 85, 95, 105, 107, 110, 183, 184, 202n.15;
 moon, names of, 50
Goff, Beatrice Laura, 12
Goodale, Jane C., 57
government: authoritarian, 22; devel-
 opment of, 33–34, 34, 47; empire
 building as, 8, 41, 197n.12
Grahn, Judy, 57, 62–63, 140
Great Mother, The (Neumann), 4
Greece: androgyny in, 163; dichotomy of
 good and evil in, 85–86; *hieros gamos*
 of, 61–62, 159; male power in, 185;
 rationality of, 86, 112
Gudea, king, 181

Halaf culture, 25, 27–28, 29, 83
Hall, Mark, 17, 50, 51, 61, 70, 71
Hallo, William W., 6, 8, 17, 49, 51, 63,
 65, 69, 71, 73, 90, 181, 182
Hammurabi, Code of, 40
Harris, Rivkah, 19, 151, 164
Hassuna culture, 25–26
hat, as worn by high priestesses, *14,* 40
headdress, bitumen, 29
Hebrews: goddesses of, 85, 185; mono-
 theism of, 84, 85, 185